JOSEPH CONRAD

JOSEPH CONRAD

A Personal Remembrance

By

FORD MADOX FORD

(FORD MADOX HUEFFER)

JOINT AUTHOR WITH JOSEPH CONRAD OF "ROMANCE",
"THE INHERITORS", "THE NATURE OF A CRIME", ETC., ETC.

"For it would be delightful to catch the echo of the desperate,
earnest and funny quarrels which enlivened those old days."
JOSEPH CONRAD.

THE ECCO PRESS
New York

First published in 1989 by
The Ecco Press
26 West 17th Street
New York, N.Y. 10011

Reprinted by special arrangement with Janice Biala,
Executrix of the Ford Madox Ford Estate

Library of Congress Cataloging-in-Publication Data
Ford, Ford Madox, 1873-1939.
Joseph Conrad, a personal remembrance.
Reprint. Originally published:
New York: Octagon Books, 1965.
1. Conrad, Joseph, 1857-1924—Biography.
2. Conrad, Joseph, 1857-1924—Friends and associates.
3. Ford, Ford Madox, 1873-1939—Friends and associates.
4. Novelists, English—20th century—Biography.
I. Title.
PR6005.04Z72   1989   823'.912 [B]   88-31085

ISBN 0-88001-176-9

Printed in the United States of America

PREFACE

Nine years ago the writer had occasion to make a hasty will. Since one of the provisions of this document appointed Conrad the writer's literary executor, we fell to discussing the question of literary biographies in general and our own in particular. We hit, as we generally did, very quickly upon a formula, both having a very great aversion to the usual official biography for men of letters whose lives are generally uneventful. But we agreed that should a writer's life have interests beyond the mere writing upon which he had employed himself, this life might well be the subject of a monograph. It should then be written by an artist and be a work of art. To write: "Joseph Conrad Korzeniowski was born on such a day of such a year in the town of 'So and So' in the Government of Kieff", *and so to continue would not conduce to such a rendering as this great man desired. So, here, to the measure of the ability vouchsafed, you have a projection of Joseph Conrad as, little by little, he revealed himself to a human being during many years of close intimacy. It is so that, by degrees, Lord Jim appeared to Marlowe, or that every human soul by degrees appears to every other human soul. For, according to our view of the thing, a novel should be the biography of a man or of an affair, and a biography, whether of a man or an affair, should be a novel, both being, if they are efficiently performed, renderings of such affairs as are our human lives.*

This then is a novel, not a monograph; a portrait, not a narration: for what it shall prove to be worth, a work of art, not a compilation. It is conducted exactly along the lines laid down by us, both for the novel which is biography and for the biography which is a novel. It is the rendering of an affair intended first of all to make you see the subject in his scenery. It contains no documentation at all; for it no dates have been looked up; even all the quotations but two have been left unverified, coming from the writer's memory. It is the writer's impression of a writer who avowed himself impressionist. Where the writer's memory has proved to be at fault over a detail afterwards out of curiosity looked up, the writer has allowed the fault to remain on the page; but as to the truth of

PREFACE

the impression as a whole, the writer believes that no man would care — or dare — to impugn it. It *was that that Joseph Conrad asked for: the task has been accomplished with the most pious scrupulosity.* For something human was to him dearer than the wealth of the Indies.

GUERMANTES, SEINE ET MARNE, August.
BRUGES, October, 1924.

CONTENTS

Part I
"C'EST TOI QUI DORS DANS L'OMBRE"

I

HE was small rather than large in height; very broad in the shoulder and long in the arm; dark in complexion with black hair and a clipped black beard. He had the gestures of a Frenchman who shrugs his shoulders frequently. When you had really secured his attention he would insert a monocle into his right eye and scrutinise your face from very near as a watchmaker looks into the works of a watch. He entered a room with his head held high, rather stiffly and with a haughty manner, moving his head once semicircularly. In this one movement he had expressed to himself the room and its contents; his haughtiness was due to his determination to master that room, not to dominate its occupants, his chief passion being the realisation of aspects to himself.

In the Pent Farm, beneath the South Downs, there was a great kitchen with a wavy brick floor. On this floor sat a great many cats; they were needed to keep down rats and they got some milk of a morning. Every morning a wild robin with a red breast and greenish-khaki body would hop, not fly, across the floor of the kitchen between the waiting cats. The cats would avert their glances, pulsing their sheathed claws in and out. The robin would hop through the inner doorway of the kitchen, across an angle of the low dining-room and so up the bedroom stairs. When the maid with the morning letters and the tea tray opened the bedroom door the robin would fly through the low, dark room and perch on a comb, stuck into a brush on the dressing table, against the long, low, leaded windows. It awaited crumbs of bread and tiny morsels of lump sugar from the tea tray. It had never been taught to go on these adventures. This robin attended at the opening of the first letter that, more than a quarter of a century ago, the writer received from Joseph Conrad. The robin watched with its beady eyes the sheet of blue-grey paper with the large rather ornamental handwriting. . . . It was afterwards drowned in a cream jug which took away from its aspect of a supernatural visitant.

Above the large kitchen was the large Men's Room where the hinds of the farm had been used to sleep. It was entered by a ladder which was removed at night so that the hinds should not murder the farmer or do worse to the farmer's wife. The low windows of this low room were leaded in diamond shapes, the glass frosted with the green of great age. One of these windows had inscribed upon it, no doubt by a diamond, the name *John Kemp* and the date 1822. Conrad always objected to *John Kemp* as a name not sufficiently aristocratic for the hero of "Romance", who was the grandson of an earl, but the writer liked it and it remained so in the book.

Years before that, looking through the pages of Dickens's "All the Year Round" for woodcuts contributed by Ford Madox Brown, upon whose biography he had been engaged, the writer had come upon a short rendering of the official account of the trial of Aaron Smith. This had been the last trial for piracy that had ever been held at the Old Bailey and the prisoner was acquitted. The story told by him in the dock was sufficiently that of "Romance", as it now stands. It struck the writer at once after the reading of the first few paragraphs — that here indeed was what we used to call a *subject*, with a tone of voice as if the word had been italicised. For certain subjects will grip you with a force almost supernatural, as if something came from behind the printed, the written or the spoken word, or from within the aura of the observed incident in actual life,

and caught you by the throat, really saying: "Treat
me." So in the dusky air of the British Museum
Reading Room, whilst that first perusal was being
made, it was almost as if the genie of the place
exclaimed, "Treat this subject." If you do it will
mean fortune; if not, lifelong ill-luck. It brought
fortune.

The first treatment of that story by the writer
was of an incredible thinness. It was like the
whisper of a nonagenarian and the writer had
tried to make it like the whisper of a nonagenarian.
It was finished just before, in 1898 or so, Conrad
first came to see the writer at Limpsfield. . . .
Why the writer should ever have thought of writing of pirates, heaven knows, or why, having determined to write of pirates it should have been
his ambition to treat them as if in terms of a very
faded manuscript of a Greek play! But that was
certainly his ambition and, as it proved, his ambition was certainly granted to him to achieve.
Every sentence had a dying fall and every paragraph faded out. The last sentences of that original draft ran: *Above our heads a nightingale*
(did something; *poured out its soul*, as like as not,
or *poured out its melody on the summer air*, the
cadence calling there for eleven syllables). *As it
was June it sang a trifle hoarsely.* . . . The reader

will observe that the writer had then already read his "Trois Contes", just as the first words of Conrad's first book were pencilled on the flyleaves and margins of "Madame Bovary." The last cadences, then, of Herodias run: "*Et tous trois, ayant pris la tète de Jokanaan s'en allaient vers Galilé. Comme elle était très lourde, ils la portaient alternativement.*" . . . As cadence the later sentences are an exact pastiche of the former. In each the first contains nineteen syllables; the concluding one commences with "As it was", and is distinguished by the *u* sounds of "*June*" and "*lourd*" and the *or* sounds of "*hoarse*" and "*portaient.*" It was in that way that, before the writer and Conrad met, they had studied their Flaubert. . . .

Conrad came round the corner of the house carrying a small child; that did not impede his slightly stiff gait and the semicircular motion of his head as he took in the odd residence, the lettuces protected by wire netting from the rabbits, or the immense view that lay before the cottage. He was conducted by Mr. Edward Garnett. In those days the writer had been overcome by one of those fits of agricultural enthusiasm that have overwhelmed him every few years, so that such descriptive writers as have attended to him have given you his picture in a startling alternation as a Piccadilly dude in top hat, morning coat and spats, and as an extremely dirty agricultural labourer. Mr. Garnett lived an acre or so up the hill; Mr. Conrad and his family were staying on Limpsfield Chart. It was in those days Mr. Garnett's ambition to appear what the French call *lézardé:* he might have been a very, a very long lizard, indistinguishable, save for his spectacles, from the monstrous stones of his cavernous and troglodytic residence. From his mansion the writer's two-roomed cottage might have been a volcanic fragment, thrown off. Mr. Garnett frequently reproved the writer for wearing dark grey frieze. It caused, he said, a blot on the Limpsfield hillside into whose tones one should sink. The writer was engrossed in carrying out experiments, suggested by Professor Gressent of the Sorbonne in Paris. He was trying to make ten lettuces grow where before had been ten thousand nettles and was writing articles for the *Outlook* on the usage of the potato as an extirpator of thistles, in sand. That is accepted as good farming now.

—❈—

Upon the writer Conrad made no impression at all. Mr. Conrad was the author of "Almayer's Folly", a great book of a romantic fashion, but written too much in the style of Alphonse Daudet, whom the writer had outgrown at school, knowing the " Lettres de Mon Moulin " at eighteen by heart. A great, new writer then. But as to great writers or artists this writer even then *en avait soupé*, cradled in the proof sheets of Rossetti, with Swinburne, Watts-Dunton, Hall Caine (Sir Something Hall Caine) and all the Pre-Raphaelites for the commonest objects of his landscape. And Mr. Garnett used to lead the Great New, one by one, to poke up the writer as if he had been a mangey lion. The writer no doubt roared. In that way Mr. Garnett led up Stephen Crane, Conrad, Lord Ollivier, now H.B.M. Minister for India, the wife of the Secretary of the Fabian Society, the Secretary of the Fabian Society. . . . A whole procession; precisely as if one had been a mangey lion in a travelling menagerie. Or perhaps a man at the zoo! And Mr. Garnett would do the poking up, telling the distinguished that the writer was possessed of too much individuality ever to find readers. . . . It was the most depressing period of a life not lacking in depressing periods.

The writer perhaps roared. Obviously the writer roared on that occasion, but he certainly rather disliked Conrad as you dislike those who pass before your cage and get you poked up. We went afterwards with several children up to the sloping lawn of Mr. Garnett's residence. It is at that point that a real remembrance of this beautiful genius comes to the writer. . . . One of the children crawled over the sloping grass as weak new-born kittens crawl; another, on the other hand, with an engrossed face, a little older, whilst Conrad stuck his eyeglass into his eye, progressed for all the world like a *cul de jatte* of our Paris streets. Two fists stuck into the ground, one short leg projected, the other curled underneath, blonde and determined, it levered itself over the grass with its hands and between its arms. And Conrad threw back his head and laughed; his eyeglass fell out; he stuck it in his eye again and gazed at the child; threw back his head and roared, and uttered odd words in Marseilles French. . . . Immediately afterwards Mr. Garnett assured Mr. Conrad for the third time that the writer was too individual ever to have a public for his writings. It was of course high praise. . . .

So the writer left Limpsfield and returned to the Pent Farm. A complete veil dropped between himself and Conrad. And then suddenly came the letter at whose reading the robin attended. The writer had indeed roared at Limpsfield. Obviously he had told Conrad the story of John-Kemp-Aaron-Smith, for Conrad asked him to consider the idea of a collaboration over that story — which Mr. Garnett had told him was too individual ever to find even a publisher. It would otherwise have been an impertinence on the part of Conrad. And Conrad was never impertinent. His politeness even to his grocer was always Oriental.

The writer's answer was the obvious one that Conrad had better come and see for himself what he had let himself in for. And Conrad came. But that time *Conrad* came. . . . He was like the Sultan of the True Believers walking into a slave market. And for the writer that he remained until his lamentable death. He was a gentleman-adventurer who had sailed with Drake. Elizabethan: it was that that he was. He has been called Slav; he has been called Oriental; he has been called a Romantic. He was none of these except on the surface, to his grocer; a man has to have a surface to present to his grocer or to afternoon callers. He himself was just Man: *homo europeaus sapiens*, attuned to the late sixteenth century. In all the world he would have loved nothing better than to singe the King of Spain's beard if it had not been to write a good book. Well, he outwitted the Dutch navy in Malaysia and wrote the greatest books in the world.

—*—

He had an extraordinary old mare with such long ears that you took her for a mule. She was called Nancy. And a black wickerwork chaise. And he cared for these things with the lively passion of a man; what he had must be shipshape: reins, bit, headstall, feed. . . . I remember once in an inn yard at Winchelsea an enormous, fat, six-feet-two, lousy, greyish scoundrel of a stableman; leaning back against a wall he was, his face quivering, the colour of billsticker's paste. He panted, "I've heard tell of the British liaon; but protect me from the Rooshian bear. . . ." Russian being as near as he could get to Polish. Conrad had been talking to him; he had been stealing the mare's feed of oats. . . .

—*—

With a hyper-sensitiveness to impressions the writer, too, remembers Conrad throwing teacups into the fireplace during a discussion over the divine right of kings — a discussion with a lady who alleged light-heartedly that Marie Antoinette had been guilty of treason to France. The whole of the discussion the writer did not hear because he was discoursing to a very deaf gentleman on the genealogical tree of the Dering family.

Nor indeed can Conrad have thrown the teacups into the fire since on going away the lady said, "What a *charming* man Mr. Conrad is! I must see him often."

It was in short the passion of Conrad that you noticed first and that passion he applied to his writing: his darkness, his wide gestures, his eyes in which the light was like the glow of a volcano. This is not over-writing; his personality deserved these tributes. It was chivalry too. After his discussion with the lady over the divine right of kings he was pale, exhausted, panting almost. That was because he remembered Marie Antoinette in the Conciergerie, so ill-clad, so deprived of her children, so pallid and unkempt that to him she was real and he remembered her. And she was dead and a cheerfully heartless fine lady should not make fun—which was what it amounted to—of dead queens. Dog should not eat dog; fine ladies in silks should not gnaw the reputations of ladies fine that once wore finer silks and were now dead. It was the want of imagination in all humanity, thus in little summed up and presented to him, that aroused in him such passion and called for such self-control. For it is to be hoped that it is apparent that it was only to the writer that the impression remained of teacups thrown into the fireplace. The writer has seen Conrad just so enraged when the Bishop of London, returning from St. Petersburg after Bloody Monday, remarked that Russians would always have troubles until they were inculcated with the hearty British love of field games! He detested Russians; his passion was rather for Bonapartists than for the Bourbons, but that imbecilities should be uttered as to the lot of the suffering maddened him.   ⸺

It is characteristic of Conrad — it is most characteristic of Conrad — that when, after five years, he and the writer got to the last paragraphs of " Romance " and when the writer had written, " *For suffering is the lot of man* ", Conrad should have added, " *but not inevitable failure or worthless despair which is without end: suffering the mark of manhood which bears within its pain the hope of felicity, like a jewel set in iron.* " He had the mark of manhood!

⸺

He came then to the Pent to see what he was in for. He came in for passion — and suffering. The writer has seldom seen such suffering as was gone through by Conrad during the reading of that first draft of " Romance." Conrad had expected a drama of Cuban pirates, immense and gloomy, like "Salammbo", with a reddish illumination, passing as it were upon a distant stage. . . . For the first chapter or two — those passing at the Pent Farm — he was silent. Then he became — silent. For he seemed to have about him a capacity for as it were degrees of intensity of his silence. No doubt he listened to the first pages with a movement or so to light a cigarette, with a relaxing of the limbs or a change in the position in the chair. These must gradually have ceased.

—✻—

The parlour at the Pent was a deep room with a beam across the middle of the low ceiling; small, pink monthly roses always showed insignificant blooms that looked over the window sills. An immense tythe barn with a great, thatched, black mossy roof filled in the whole view if you sat by the fireplace; occasionally you would see a rat progressing musingly over this surface. If you approached the window you saw a narrow lawn running to a low brick wall after which the level dropped to a great stockyard floored usually with straw and not unusually with a bullock or two in it. Conrad and the writer planted an orange tree, grown from a pip, under the low north wall of this narrow garden. It was still alive in nineteen-seventeen, growing just up to the coping of the low wall where its progress was cut off by the north wind. It was a very quiet, simple room.

The writer sat in the grandfather's chair, his back to the window, beside the fireplace, reading, his manuscript held up to the light; Conrad sat forward on a rush-bottomed armchair, listening intently. (For how many years did the writer and Conrad not sit there like that!)

⁂

We began that reading after lunch of a shortish day; the lamps were brought in along with the tea. During that interval Conrad showed nervous and depressed; sunk in on himself and hardly answering questions. Conrad being then almost a stranger, this was the writer's first experience of to what Conrad's depression over an artistic problem could amount: it was like a strong current that operated on a whole roomful. . . . With his back, then, to the lamp, and Conrad completely in the shadow, the writer read on, just having the impression that his hearer's limbs were all bunched together in his chair and that they contracted gradually. There were many strong shadows in the low room where most of the light was on the ceiling.

⁂

Conrad began to groan. . . . It was by then fairly apparent to the writer that Conrad dis-

approved of the treatment of the adventures of
John Kemp; at any rate in Cuba; and the writer
had a sufficient sense already of Conrad's tempera-
ment to be disinclined to ask whether his guest
were ill. He feels now the sense of as it were
dumb obstinacy with which he read on into those
now vocal shadows in the fireside warmth. . . .
The interruptions grew in length of ejaculation.
They became, "O! O! . . . O God, my dear
Hueffer. . . ." . . . And towards the end, "O
God, my dear *faller*, how is it possible. . . ."
The writer finished with the statement that, as it
was June, the nightingale sang a trifle hoarsely.
This zoölogical observation, in spite of the ca-
dence, gave the final touch to Conrad's dejection.
The writer's voice having stopped he exclaimed,
"What? What? What's that?" When he heard
that that was the end he groaned and said, "Good
God!"—for the last time. There are writers—
French writers—who can keep the final revelation
of a whole long novel back until the last three
words. For this he had hoped. The writer would
rather have died than have so machined a book.

Conrad was the most unrivalled hatcher of
schemes for sudden and unlimited wealth or for
swift and undying glory. To see him go upon
one of these adventures was heartening in itself.

His face lit up, his muscles tautened, he first expatiated on his idea and then set out. Obviously his training as a master mariner inveigling unwilling Eastern traders into shipping cargoes that they did not want to consign, at prices that they did not want to pay, to bottoms commanded by Conrad, for one reason or another unsuited to their merchandise — this training helped him with direct human negotiations. To see him, leaning over a counter, persuading the stolid Mr. Dan West, grocer of Hythe, to grant him credit unheard of in that market town, was a singular study in fascination. The bearded, blinking and very excellent grocer — I wish I knew his equal elsewhere — understood possibly the transaction which contained in its essence bills at three months, mortgages I daresay on life insurances — heaven knows what! — and then a triumphant progress to the White Hart where the benign, dark, statuesque and really beautiful Miss Cobay presided in the dimmer recess of that very old tavern. . . . And there sat the grocer, benevolent, pleased, blinking a little, a solid, wealthy, fiftyish man, several times mayor of his ancient town, with great knowledge of men, quietly indulgent to the romantic visitor who had descended upon him. . . . For all the world he might have been the Stein of "Lord Jim" contemplating the hero of that wonderful work and saying within himself, "Romantic! . . . That's what he is—romantic!" . . . And the beautiful, statuesque, slow-moving Miss Cobay, invariably silent. The writer at least never heard her utter one word, except that, years after, motoring through that ancient Cinque Port, the writer, for old sake's sake, took a drink at the bar of the White Hart, and Miss Cobay with her enigmatic gaze asked after Mr. Conrad, then many years gone from the Pent, for all the world like one of the silent women of Conrad's early books: the heroine of "Falk" who never utters *one* word. . . . The writer, alas, alas, seems to become Marlowe.

Conrad was Conrad because he was his books. It was not that he made literature: he was literature, the literature of the Elizabethan Gentleman Adventurer. . . . Think of setting out in an old wickerwork chaise drawn by what appeared to be a mule to persuade a Hythe grocer to give you three years' credit. . . . Think of setting out from Stamford-le-Hope, a safe harbour where at least there was contact with ships, estuaries, tideways, islands, into an unknown hinterland of savage and unknown populations, of bare downs, out of sight of the refuge of the sea, to persuade an unknown wielder of the pen, the finest stylist in England, to surrender his liberty to a sailing partnership—

to surrender too his glamourous "subject", for
all the world as if you had adventured into the
hinterlands behind Palembang to ask some one
only just known to give up to you for joint working the secret of one of those mysterious creeks
where gold is found. An adventure like that of
"Victory" itself. . . . And then to insult the
owner of the creek with groans, sighs, O God's,
contortions. . . . Well, all we who supported
Conrad to his final, so great victory, were the sub-
ordinate characters of his books, putting up with
his extortionate demands for credit, for patience
or for subjects. . . . The Steins, the Whalleys,
the captain MacWhirrs . . . and now the Mar-
lowes!

—*—

For, for some hours of that distant day of our
"Romance", the reader may be assured that the
question of the very existence of that work hung
in the balance. It was truly as if Rumpelstiltkin
had come to carry off the Queen's child. (*The
dwarf*, Conrad quotes Grimm in his epigraph,
*answered, "No, something human is dearer to me
than all the wealth of the Indies!"*) The writer,
please let the reader be assured, has always been
supremely indifferent to the fate of his books; to
the estimation in which they were held—by any
soul but Joseph Conrad; to such things as career;

personal reputation and the rest. Conrad could hardly have selected a better discoverer of creeks to whom to go. But the writer was not then ignorant of the vicissitudes of human life and of literary partnerships. The terrible wrangles between Henley and the relicts and executors of Stevenson were at that moment filling the press. Or one might remember the effects on Johnson's fame, of Boswell. To do what Conrad then imperiously desired, to surrender the creek to a joint partnership was . . . asking for it!

It hung then in the balance. But there gradually appeared after dinner, through a long farm-house night until two in the morning, the magic. It was magic! There had been disclosures. Conrad had artlessly expounded his desires. Hearing, at Limpsfield, the writer develop his miraculous "subject" — of Aaron Smith, last pirate ever to be tried at the Old Bailey, of the Creek with Rio Media at the bottom of it and the pirate schooners with Nikola el Escoces in command sailing out to the sack of brig *Victoria* with her cargo of logwood, rum, raw sugar and dyes — Conrad had imagined a robust book, with every drop of the subject squeezed out of it. Whereas it was characteristic of the writer that though in the trial Aaron Smith had deposed to a lady bearing the

glamourous name of Seraphina Riego, daughter
of a *juez de la premiera instancia*, known as the
Star of Cuban Law, and inhabiting the pirate city
of Rio Media in Cuba, the writer had very carefully left out this lady in the first draft of his book,
the lady with whom John Kemp sat under the
hoarse nightingale having been a carefully dimmed
figure with bare shoulders and a handkerchief,
called Veronica. . . . Conrad had expected to
hear a reading by the finest stylist in England
of a work, far-flung in popularity as "Treasure
Island" but as "written" as "Salammbo", by the
addition to which of a few touches of description,
sea atmosphere, mists, riggings and the like, in a
fortnight, fortune should lie at the feet of the
adventurers. . . . It was another of those magic
enterprises. . . . Alas, after five years' work there
was "Romance" with its *succès d'estime*. Not
much of that, even, for the critics of our favoured
land do not believe in collaboration.

Conrad's marvellous play and change of features
came now into the story. Ruffled, the writer, even
before dinner had explained the nature of the *tour
de force* he had attempted. This was the narrative of a very old man, looking back upon that
day of his romance — as to-day this narrator looks
back. You are getting the real first draft of

"Romance" now. This is how in truth it comes out according to the technical scheme then laid down by us two.

Before dinner, then, Conrad listened to the writer's apologia with a certain frigid deference. Of course if that was the way of it, no doubt. . . . But why choose such a subject? . . . A man of sixty-two. . . . Yes, yes, of course. . . . He remained however shut up in the depth of his disappointment and still more in his reprobation of the criminal who could take hold of such a theme and not, gripping it by the throat, extract from it every drop of blood and glamour. . . . He disliked the writer as a criminal, fortune thrown away, a Book turned into the dry bone of a technical feat. He exclaimed, "Let me look at it. Let me look at the manuscript"; shuffled the leaves distastefully as if they had been the evidence of a crime. . . . To throw away fortune — that was not shipshape: to murder a subject — that was murder, foul, unnatural. . . . The dinner bell rang. . . .

At dinner there were ladies; gradually the depressed Conrad became Conrad. Pepper came under discussion. He declaimed as to how the greatest wars in the world had been fought for pepper. The Spice Islands, the East, came into

the room for a little while, with Wapping Old
Stairs, the tents of the army over Constantinople
at the end of the Russo-Turkish War with Conrad
as a sailor before the mast on the deck of a Messageries Maritimes transport. There ensued a
desperate wrangle as to whether saffron had any
flavour—in the course of the consumption of
curry. Conrad declared that saffron had no flavour; the writer, that saffron was one of the most
strongly flavoured of all possible herbs. Conrad
swore that he had carried whole cargoes of saffron;
he had spent his life in carrying cargoes of saffron;
he had known no other pursuits. The writer on
the other hand had given more saffron to diseased
poultry than ever Conrad had carried and had in
addition reproved cooks enough to make ships'
crews for not putting sufficient saffron into *poule
au riz.* . . . Conrad declared that that was merely
to give the rice an agreeable colour. The writer
called it a most disagreeable, an offensive colour. . . . Conrad's eyes flashed dangerously; his
teeth white under his drawn-back moustache. We
both contemplated Calais Sands. . . . Some one
changed the conversation to pearls. . . .

In all our ten thousand conversations down
the years we had only these two themes over
which we quarrelled: as to the taste of saffron and

as to whether one sheep is distinguishable from another.

—❋—

After that first dinner Conrad talked, there being people present whom he found sympathetic. . . . When he talked on such occasions he was like his "The Mirror of the Sea." Indeed, a great part of his "The Mirror of the Sea" was just his talk which the writer took down in a shorthand of his own extemporising, recalling to Conrad, who was then in a state of great depression, various passages of his own relating. . . . Alas, three weeks ago, the writer drove in a black, shaken, hooded contrivance, over a country of commonplace downlands, the continuation of the Kentish downs, beyond the Channel. He went, jolted behind an extravagant female quadruped, between fields of wheat that small winds ruffled into cat's-paws. And the parallel was so intimately exact that the writer found himself saying to himself, "Well, Ford, *mon vieux*, how would you render that field of wheat?" . . . The reader must take this record of a coincidence as a sincerity. . . .

—❋—

For the days have been innumerable upon which, behind the amiable mare of Conrad's or a far less amiable Exmoor pony of the writer's,

we drove—say between 1898 and 1905—over a
country of commonplace downlands and asked
ourselves how we should render a field of ripe
corn, a ten-acre patch of blue-purple cabbage.
We would try the words in French: *sillonné, bleu-
foncé, bleu-du-roi;* we would try back into English; cast around in the back of our minds for
other French words to which to assimilate our
English and thus continue for quiet hours.

—*—

So, three weeks ago to-day—thus does one return to one's old loves!—the writer drove from
just such a ramshackle, commonplace farm building in an undistinguished country over slight hills
on a flinty bye-road and heard Conrad saying to
him, "Well, Ford, *mon vieux*, how would you
render that field of wheat?" . . . Unless you have
these details you cannot know how immensely
strong an impression this beautiful genius made
on a mind not vastly impressionable or prone to
forming affections. . . . So the writer continued
turning the matter over.

He went on thinking first of French and then
of English: "*Champs de blés que les vents faibles
sillonnaient.* . . . Cornfields. . . . No, not cornfields, because that, to Americans, signifies maize.
. . . Wheat fields. . . . Fields of wheat that the
weak . . . feeble . . . light . . . what sort of

winds, breezes, airs. . . ." There is no occupation more agreeable on a still day: it is more restful, really, than fishing in a pond. . . . "Fields
of wheat that small winds ruffled into cat's-paws.
. . . That is, of course, too literary. . . ."

—*—

These considerations remained in the front of
his mind as he was jolted over the abominable
granite setts of a small market town, to the dilapidated station. He continued to think of wheat,
dusty, bronzed, golden, as if running away over a
small hillside — whilst he purchased tickets of a
disagreeable woman behind a grille, whilst he purchased an English paper of a very agreeable woman
in a blue pinafore. On the railway platform he
said, "*Dont les vents faibles sillonnaient les sur
faces roussâtres,* . . ." whilst looking at black capital letters in the paper that his companion held
folded. It struck him at once, "This is a bad
joke. . . . That paper is of the sort that makes
bad jokes. . . . He was speaking to me. Not five,
not three . . . minutes. . . . Not three seconds;
just now on this platform . . . the duskyish voice
with the brown accent, rather caressing. . . ."

—*—

The writer exclaimed, "Look! *Look!*" . . .
His companion unfolded the paper. The announcement went across two columns in black,

leaded caps. . . . *SUDDEN DEATH OF JOSEPH CONRAD*. They were demolishing an antiquated waiting room on the opposite platform, three white-dusty men with pickaxes; a wall was all in broken zigzags. The writer said to himself, "*C'est le mur d'un silence éternel qui descend devant vous!*" There descended across the dusty wall a curtain of moonlight, thrown across by the black shadows of oak trees. We were on a verandah that had a glass roof. Under the glass roof climbed passion flowers, and vine tendrils strangled them. We were sitting in deck chairs. It was one o'clock in the morning. Conrad was standing in front of us, talking. Talking on and on, in the patches of moonlight and patches of shadow from the passion flowers and vines! The little town in which we were dominated the English channel from a low hilltop. He was wearing a dark reefer coat and white trousers.

—*—

He was talking of Malaysia, palm trees, the little wives of rajahs in coloured sarongs—or perhaps not sarongs?—crouched round him on the ground; he himself cross-legged on the ground teaching the little wives of rajahs to use sewing machines! Moored to a rotting quay—as it might have been Palembang, but of course it was not Palembang—was his schooner. His schooner had in its hold half a cargo of rifles under half a cargo of sewing machines. The rajahs, husbands of the little wives, did not like their Dutch suzerains and in that country the War has lasted not five but three hundred and fifty-five years. . . .

That then was Conrad on the occasions when he talked as he did on that first evening after dinner. His voice was then usually low, rather intimate and caressing. He began by speaking slowly, but later on he spoke very fast. His accent was precise, rather dusky, the accent of dark rather than fair races. He impressed the writer at first as a pure Marseilles Frenchman; he spoke English with great fluency and distinction, with correctitude in his syntax, his words absolutely exact as to meaning but his accentuation so faulty that he was at times difficult to understand and his use of adverbs as often as not eccentric. He used "shall" and "will" very arbitrarily. He gesticulated with his hands and shoulders when he wished to be emphatic, but when he forgot himself in the excitement of talking he gesticulated with his whole body, throwing himself about in his chair, moving his chair nearer to yours. Finally he would spring up, go to a distance, and walk back and forth across the end of the room. When the writer talked he was a very good listener, sitting rather

curled up whilst the writer walked unceasingly
back and forth along the patterned border of the
carpet.

—*—

We talked like that from about ten, when the
ladies had gone to bed, until half-past two in the
morning. We talked about Flaubert and Maupassant — sounding each other, really. Conrad
was still then inclined to have a feeling for Daudet
— for such books as "Jack." This the writer contemned with the sort of air of the superior person
who tells you that Hermitage is no longer a wine
for a gentleman. We talked of Turgenev — the
greatest of all poets; "Byelshin Prairie" from the
"Letters of a Sportsman", the greatest of all
pieces of writing; Turgenev wrapped in a cloak
lying on the prairie at night, at a little distance
from a great fire, beside which the boy horse-
tenders talked desultorily about the Roosalki of
the forests with the green hair and water nymphs
that drag you down to drown in the river.

—*—

We agreed that a poem was not that which was
written in verse but that, either prose or verse,
that had constructive beauty. We agreed that the
writing of novels was the one thing of importance
that remained to the world and that what the
novel needed was the New Form. We confessed

that each of us desired one day to write Absolute Prose.

—➤—

But that which really brought us together was a devotion to Flaubert and Maupassant. We discovered that we both had "Felicite", "St.-Julien l'Hospitalier", immense passages of "Madame Bovary", "La Nuit", "Ce Cochon de Morin" and immense passages of "Une Vie" by heart. Or so nearly by heart that what the one faltered over the other could take up. And indeed, on the last occasion when we met, in May of this year, agreeing that we had altered very little, surprisingly little —oh, not the least in the world!—the writer began, "*La nuit, balancé par l'ouragan . . .*" and Conrad went on, "*tandis que le feu grégeois ruisselait*," right down to, "*Et comme il était très fort, hardi, courageux et avisé. . . .*"

—➤—

Before we went on that earlier night to bed Conrad confessed to the writer that previous to suggesting a collaboration he had consulted a number of men of letters as to its advisability. He said that he had put before them his difficulties with the language, the slowness with which he wrote and the increased fluency that he might acquire in the process of going minutely into words with an acknowledged master of English. The

writer imagines that he had actually consulted Mr.
Edward Garnett, W. E. Henley and Mr. Marriott
Watson. Of these the only one that Conrad mentioned was W. E. Henley. He stated succinctly
and carefully that he had said to Henley — Henley had published "The Nigger of the Narcissus"
in his *Review* — "Look here. I write with such
difficulty: my intimate, automatic, less expressed
thoughts are in Polish; when I express myself with
care I do it in French. When I write I think in
French and then translate the words of my thoughts
into English. This is an impossible process for one
desiring to make a living by writing in the English language. . . ." And Henley, according to
Conrad on that evening, had said, "Why don't
you ask H. to collaborate with you. He is the
finest stylist in the English language of to-day. . . ."
The writer, it should be remembered, though by
ten or fifteen years the junior of Conrad was by
some years his senior, at any rate as a published
author, and was rather the more successful of the
two as far as sales went.

—✱—

Henley obviously had said nothing of the sort.
Indeed, as the writer has elsewhere related, on the
occasion of a verbal duel that he had later with
Henley, that violent-mouthed personality remarked
to him, "Who the hell are you? I never even

heard your name!" or words to that effect. It probably does not very much matter. What had no doubt happened was that Conrad had mentioned the writer's name to Henley and Henley had answered, "I daresay he'll do as well as any one else." No, it probably does not matter, except as a light on the character and methods of Conrad, and as to his ability to get his own way. . . .

For it was obviously *une émotion forte* that the writer received in those small hours in a sufficiently dim farmhouse room. In such affairs Conrad's caressing, rather dragging voice would take on a more Polish intonation and would drop. His face would light up; it was as if he whispered; as if we both whispered in a conspiracy against a sleeping world. And no doubt that was what it was. The world certainly did not want us, not at that date; and to be reputed the finest English stylist was enough, nearly, to get you sent to gaol. Something foreign, that was what it was. . . .

At any rate when, with a flat candlestick, the writer at last showed his guest into a shadowy, palely papered, coldish bedroom and closed the door on him, he felt as if a king were enclosed within those walls. A king-conspirator: a sovereign-Pretender; Don Carlos of a world whose subjects are shadows.

II

As for what happened immediately to the history of "Romance", the book, the writer's mind preserves a complete blank! It might be easy to construct images out of probabilities or by consultation with one person or another. But that would not be within the spirit of the bond; this is the record of the impression made by Conrad the Impressionist upon another writer, impressionist also. It is an offering In Memoriam constructed solely out of memory.

＊

Some years ago Mr. H. G. Wells took occasion to write to the papers. He stated that the writer had visited him and informed him that he had persuaded Conrad to collaborate with himself. Mr. Wells' memory must almost certainly have betrayed him, though the matter is of no great importance. What does remain in the writer's mind very clearly is this. . . .

＊

The writer and Conrad made several choppings and changings in their occupation of the Pent: the writer occupied it for several years; Conrad then lived in it with the writer's spare furniture which was mostly of Pre-Raphaelite origin. It pleased Conrad to write at a Chippendale bureau on which Christina Rossetti had once written or at another which had once belonged to Thomas Carlyle: one got in those days those small, cheerful pleasures out of life. Then Conrad occupied the Pent altogether, the mournful house under the bare downs exercising a great fascination over him. When you went out of the front door — Mr. Walter Crane, who during one of our movings about Kent and Sussex took the house furnished, had painted a Japanese crane and some verses on that door — when you went out, then, the narrow garden giving on to the stockyard had a short brick path running under the windows and it was very soothing to see the flattish lines of the country running away for a great distance, one convolution going into another. The brick path dried up very quickly in the wettest of weathers; up and down it, as if on a quarterdeck, Conrad would pace for hours and hours, the lines of the country soothing him. In that part of England the words of Charles II are most true; what with the shelter of the downs and the position near the sea, there is there scarcely any day upon which a man may not go abroad — at any rate to the extent of a brick path under his windows. The great barn closed in the scene immediately to the front, but you saw the fields to the right, so it was a very quiet and private place. . . . And indeed, during the last of our conversations, this year, Conrad alluded to the fact that, for the first time in his life, he had, in his vastly more arranged residence of that day, a study to himself. And he added, "Ah, but it isn't the *Pent!*" He said too that the great tythe barn had been burned down during threshing.

—⋆—

We used in our day to take great entertainment out of shooting rats with a Flobert rifle from the brick path. There were channels made by these animals in the black-green thatch of the barn and you would see them proceeding leisurely from end to end of the great expanse in broad daylight. Then. . . . Whiff would go the Flobert and the small bullet pinging into the thatch would send a rat bounding away over the corrugations in the old straw into some hole, for all the world with the action of a tiger bounding over watercourses. As far as memory serves we never hit a rat: but one notable success was scored to the writer. Fired at from an incredible distance—ninety yards or so, something gigantic!—a great old grey rat crossing a road collapsed feebly. We ran forward and dispatched it with the butt. That was ever afterwards scored to the writer as an immense feat of marksmanship, often referred to. If any one talked of shooting Conrad would say, "Ah, but you should have seen Ford's shot at the rat! . . ." Actually the writer, with a little more farm knowledge, was sure that the rat was dying of old age before it was fired at, the bullet never reaching it. But he has kept his own counsel to this day of confession. . . . No, we were not high-brow there at the Pent. We played dominoes, Conrad with passion and the skill of a master. Indeed, in how many city Meccas and Belgian cafés must we not have rattled the black and white bones over round, white marble table tops! We played écarté or, when very serious, chess, but usually dominoes, at which the writer never remembers to have won a game. Sometimes the writer knocked a golf ball about the fields, Conrad, standing on the brick path, regarding the occupation with the contempt, say, that his collaborator bestowed on Daudet. Once the writer seriously sat down to describe in words the satisfaction you feel when you have brought off a good drive and see the white ball lyrically against the blue sky. It was a careful piece of writing, *mots justes* and all. Conrad looked at it with attention and then slowly, blankly raised his shoulders and eyebrows, we returning to dominoes.

III

On one of those days, then, we drove in state from the Pent to pay a call on Mr. Wells at Sandgate. There was a curious incident. As we stood on the doorstep of Mr. Wells' villa, in the hesitant mind of those paying a state call, behold, the electric bell-push, all of itself, went in and the bell sounded. . . . Conrad exclaimed, "*Tiens!* . . . The Invisible Man!" and burst into incredible and incredulous laughter. In the midst of it the door opened before grave faces.

—*—

We paid our call. Whether we were taken to be drunk or no only the owners of those grave faces can say. I suppose that we were. But the incident of the bell-pull was of a nature that had a peculiar appeal to Conrad's humour. For years after, a translation of Mr. Wells' book having appeared in Italian, you could never mention that author's name without Conrad saying, "*Tiens!* . . . *L'Uomo Invisible!*" . . . Indeed, during a visit in an interval of our long separation caused by European vicissitudes and their sequelæ Conrad asked the writer, "Do you ever see Wells now?"

and added, "*L'Uomo Invisible*. . . . Do you remember?"

⟶✶⟵

But Mr. Wells' "The Invisible Man" made an extremely marked impression on Conrad, as indeed it did on the writer. So it deserved to. Indeed, as far as memory serves, "The Invisible Man", the end of the "Sea Lady" and some phrases that that book contained, and two short stories called "The Man Who Could Work Miracles" and "Fear", made up at that date all the English writing that, acting as it were as a junta, we absolutely admired. Later there came the stories of Mr. Cunninghame Graham, the writing of W. H. Hudson and — with reservations on the part of Conrad for the later novels — the work of Henry James.

⟶✶⟵

It was as if, when we considered any other English writer's work, we always in the end said, "Ah, but do you remember 'Ce Cochon de Morin'?" or the casquette of Charles Bovary, according to the type of work undergoing commendation. After reading the passage, say, of the pavior striking with the spade at the invisibility flying past him from "The Invisible Man", or the episode of the turning over of the lamp and the burning downwards, from "The Man Who Could Work Mira-

cles ", we recalled no French masterpiece. . . .
These pieces were authentic, in construction, in
language and in the architectural position occupied by them in the book or story — in the progression of the effect!

Mr. Wells has recorded that he was aware that
at this date there was a conspiracy going on at the
Pent against himself and against British literature.
Against British literature there was, if you choose
to call it so; against Mr. Wells the extent of our
machinations is as recorded above.

Conrad had odd, formal notions of how one
should proceed in the life literary. As far as he
was concerned the purpose of our call on Mr.
Wells was to announce to the world of letters that
we were engaged in collaboration. To the writer
this was just exactly a matter of indifference except for a not materially pronounced disinclination
to pay calls anywhere or at any time. But Conrad liked proceedings of a State nature. He would
have liked the driving in a barouche to pay calls
on Academicians such as is practised by candidates
for membership of the French Academy. And
exceedingly vivid in the writer's mind is the feeling he had, as we drove down the sloping railway
bridge above Sandling Junction. He was like a

brown paper parcel on a seat beside a functionary in a green uniform, decorated with golden palm leaves and a feathered cocked hat. . . .

—✳—

We were then going over the third draft of the second part of "Romance" and had at last finally and psychologically decided that the book would eventually go on. Of this the writer is certain. He is certain because the exact image and air of that time came back to him suddenly whilst making a very minute recension of the text of the French translation of "Romance." The writer was in mid-ocean on the deck of a liner, reading very meticulously the translation of an episode which related how, on a blue night in Kingston Vale, John Kemp knocked down, in the presence of the Admiral of the Fleet in the Jamaica waters, a Mr. Topnambo, member of the Governor's Council, who wore white trousers that glimmered in the half-light. . . . There were on that upper deck in the sunlight a number of New York Jews playing pinocle and a number of Washington flappers reading novels. But the writer heard his own voice as, in the low parlour of the Pent, he read aloud the passage that concerned Mr. Topnambo, the blue night, the white trousers, the barouches standing in the moonlight waiting for Admiral Rowley and his intoxicated following to

take the road. And then Conrad, interrupting. . . .
" By Jove," he said, "it's a third person who is
writing!"

-*-

The psychology of that moment is perfectly
plain to the writer. Conrad interrupted with a
note of relief in his voice. He had found a formula
to justify collaboration in general and our collaboration. Until then we had struggled tacitly each
for our own note in writing. With the coming of
blue nights, the moon, palms and the brilliant lights
of the inn reflected down the river, Conrad saw the
possibilities that there were for his own exotic note
in the story. Above all, with the coming of politics;
for John Kemp, in coming to blows with Mr. Topnambo, member of the Governor's Council, then
and there identified himself with the party in the
island of Jamaica that at that date desired annexa-
tion by the United States.

-*-

This at once made our leading character handle-
able by Conrad. John Kemp merely kidnapped
by pirates and misjudged by the judicial bench of
our country was not so vastly attractive, but a John
Kemp who was in addition a political refugee,
suspect of High Treason and victim of West India
merchants. . . . That was squeezing the last drop
of blood out of the subject. . . .

The differences in our temperaments were sufficiently well marked. Conrad was brave: he was
for inclusion and hang the consequences. The
writer, more circumspect, was for ever on the
watch to suppress the melodramatic incident and
the sounding phrase. So, till that psychological
moment, the writer doing most of the first drafting,
Conrad had been perpetually crying, "Give!
Give!" The writer was to give one more, and one
more, and again one more turn to the screw that
sent the rather listless John Kemp towards an inevitable gallows. The actual provision of intrigue
in 1820 between England and Jamaica was the
writer's business. Conrad contented himself with
saying, "You must invent. You have got to make
that fellow live perpetually under the shadow of
the gallows." In the original draft of the book John
Kemp had been the mere second mate of a merchant ship going out to Jamaica in the ordinary
course of his business of following the sea. But in
the second draft he was mixed up with smugglers
and fled from Hythe beach in the moonlight with
the Bow Street runners hot on his trail—already
a candidate for the professional attentions of the
hangman. In that second draft, however, he was
in Jamaica, still merely a planter's apprentice—
insufficiently hangable. There had to be more
inevitability in the shape of invention. The writer

therefore set to work to read a vast number of
Jamaica newspapers of the twenties and, finding
that that island was then an ant-heap of intrigue
by what were called Secessionists, it was an easy
task to identify Kemp hangably with those traitors
to the British crown.   Conrad, however, was a
Loyalist: a Loyalist to every régime that ever existed but passionately a Loyalist to Great Britain.
It was therefore necessary to give the screw one
turn more: Kemp had to be made a misjudged
man, betrayed by the stupid cruelty of merchants
and the administration.   He thus became exactly
a figure for Conrad to handle.   For, if Conrad
were the eternal Loyalist, nevertheless the unim-
aginative and cruel stupidity of Crown and Government officials was an essential part of his creed.
He was a politician — but a politician of the *im-
passe*.   The British Empire was for him the perfection of human perfections, but *all* its politicians,
all its public officials, police, military officers of
the Crown, gaolers, pilots, port admirals and
policies were of an imbecility that put them in intelligence below the first lieutenant of the French
navy that you could come across. . . .

So, by that moment, we had worked John Kemp
into a position that can have been occupied by very
few unjustly accused heroes of romance.   When

he stood in the Old Bailey Dock he had the whole legal, the whole political, the whole naval forces of the Crown, the whole influence at once of the City of London and of the Kingdom of Spain determined to hang him. And the writer is bound to confess that on reading " Romance ", after an interval of twenty years — and in a French translation! — the hairs really did rise on his scalp over the predicament of John Kemp on his trial. And he wondered at the melodramatic genius that had been possessed by that third writer that was neither himself nor Conrad. . . .

For having got hold of that comforting theory Conrad never abandoned it. At intervals during our readings aloud that lasted for years he would say, always as if it were a *trouvaille*, that *that* was certainly the writing of a third party. It had not been long before he had given up all hope of swift fortune coming with the speedy finishing of that book. For the writer the pleasure of eternal technical discussion with Conrad was a sufficient motive for continuing our labours. But for Conrad, with his stern sense of the necessity for making a career, that was not enough. He had to find at least an artistic justification for going on. We were both extremely unaccepted writers, but we could both write. What was the sense of not

writing apart if there were no commercial gain?
He found it in the æsthetically comforting thought
that the world of letters was enriched by yet a
third artist. The third artist had neither his cour-
age nor his gorgeousness; he himself had none of
his collaborator's literary circumspection or verbal
puritanism. So the combination was at least . . .
different.

⭒

Thus came about our drive to the Lower Sandgate Road. Conrad considered it appropriate that
we should make an official announcement. The
collaboration was determined upon. For the receiving of this official communication no one could
have been more appropriate than the author of
"The Invisible Man." Conrad had in those days
a very strong sense that those who had taken part
in his launching as a writer had the right to have
communicated to them any crucial determination
at which he arrived. It was a fine trait in his
character. He had originally consulted Mr. Henley, Mr. Marriott Watson and, the writer pre-
sumes, Mr. Edward Garnett, these having been,
as it were, his chief backers behind the scenes.
Mr. Wells had been his chief backer before the
public — as Reviewer. All the reviews that
"Almayer's Folly" had received had amounted to
a mountain of praise; the most tremendous and

moving commendation had been that contributed by Mr. Wells to the *Saturday Review*, an organ that was then almost miraculously regarded, under the editorship of Mr. Frank Harris. Mr. Wells then, living in our neighbourhood, to whom better could this junta have proceeded? So at least Conrad thought and the writer offered no active objection.

Mr. Wells apparently thought the same. Of what happened at that villa in the Lower Sandgate Road, except that the back garden had, descending to the sea-beach, a stepladder up and down which several charming creatures were disporting themselves with the Channel as background, the writer carries in his memory now only the conversation of Bob Stevenson and the remembrance of Conrad, talking to Mrs. Wells with enormous animation about the great storm in which for the first time he came up the Channel, passing that point. The writer was engaged in remembering that great storm. He had been at school at Folkestone on the cliff almost perpendicularly above where we then sat. In the morning after the gale had blown itself out we looked down in sunlight from the edge of the Leas. The whole sickle of Dungeness Bay had a fleet ashore on its beaches — innumerable smacks and coasting

vessels, large international sailing ships and two
East Indiamen, the *Plassy* and the *Clive,* with
their towering black and white sides, all heeling
over, rigging and canvas hanging down like cur-
tains right round the bay, unforgettable and helpless. . . . Bob Stevenson was engaged in telling
the writer with animation almost equal to that of
Conrad that Ford Madox Brown could not paint.
The writer was wishing himself with the group
round Conrad and Mrs. Wells. The crossing of
the voices of those two brilliant conversationalists
remains still in these ears, and the odd mixture of
feelings. . . .

On the next day Mr. Wells bicycled up to Aldington Knoll, where at about seven miles distant
from the Pent the writer was once again leading
an agricultural life of the severer type — in a cottage of the most minute, the Conrads occupying
the Pent. The writer was, indeed, engaging himself on the invention of a new species of potato in
the intervals of contriving the gallows for John
Kemp. Mr. Wells came to persuade the writer
not to collaborate with Conrad. With an extreme
earnestness he pleaded with the writer not to spoil
Conrad's style. "The wonderful Oriental style.
. . . It's as delicate as clockwork and you'll only
ruin it by sticking your fingers in it." The writer

answered that Conrad wanted a collaboration and as far as the writer was concerned Conrad was going to get what he wanted. He can still see the dispirited action of Mr. Wells as he mounted his bicycle by the rear step and rode away along that ridge of little hills. . . . No more than those two speeches had been exchanged.

IV

Into the still, depressed note of the Pent there had introduced itself the tremendous panorama of sea and sky that showed from Aldington with its Knoll. We passed our time driving the amiable mare or the infamous Exmoor pony between one and the other. We went out of a sunshiny morning with bits of manuscript; we returned through bitter rain-storms, the mud splashing up visibly before the dim lanthorns, the manuscript read aloud, commented on, docketed for alteration. . . . It comes back as a time of great tranquillity, though the high skies of Aldington, with the sickle-shaped, painted marsh and the flat Channel ending with the pink cliffs of Boulogne, seem cracked as the surface of an old, bright painting will be cracked — with the agonies of Conrad's poverty, unsuccess, negotiations and misgivings.

Still, a time of great tranquillities, and, at intervals, there were triumphs. Pinker, a blinking Bramah in the shape of Destiny, would grant an unimaginable advance; William Heinemann — the most generous and wise of publishers, a Jew

at that — would hand out an unexpected cheque
on the top floor of Number 31 Bedford Street
whilst the writer kept Pawling — a blond Chris-
tian but much more like a publisher than his
Semitic partner — interested as well as he might
with a description of the plot of "The Inheritors",
a thin collaboration with no plot in particular that
Heinemanns eventually published. Then Conrad
would come in, buttoning his overcoat over the
cheque; Mr. Pawling would throw up his hands
and exclaim to the writer, "You've let him get at
that ass William again. By God, that is not
cricket!" . . . And the two conspirators against
the peace of mind of Number 31 Bedford Street
would proceed to the famous Bodega just out of
the Strand. There, with Sir Henry Irving and
Nellie Farren at adjoining tables, over smoked
salmon and champagne in small tumblers, they
would play dominoes until the last train for
Sandling Junction, with its quiet lines of scenery,
its fresh breath of air, and the mare in charge of
the stable boy who would be just lighting the
lamps of the trap — that last train leaving Charing
Cross at 4.50 and getting down just at dusk. . . .

There is something conducive to writing in low
rooms, in a commonplace downland country, with
nearly level fields that run into quiet convolutions,

away to a distance. Let the direct lighting be modified by a barn, the illumination coming from the peak of the sky: let there be a quarterdeck walk up and down which Conrad may turn in his pyjamas and dressing gown occasionally, getting relief from his thoughts in a glance at the quiet fields amongst which the writer will be practising golf strokes. . . . Well, in just such a room with a barn to block the direct light, with a miniature stockyard, in a commonplace downland country the writer — sits writing! And you dare to tell him that he cannot go out and, in the rain, catch his dangerous pony that swings round and kicks the inviting sieve of corn out of your hand, just missing your chest. . . . He cannot drive the seven miles to the Pent to ask Conrad what he thinks of Colonel Marchand and Fashoda! . . . You must surely be lying. . . . Or you mean to tell him that in half an hour Conrad, in the dilapidated motor hired from the White Hart at Stamford, won't be coming in to ask what we are to think of Fashoda and Colonel Marchand and what we shall do if there is really war with France. . . . We get the London papers only by the second post at 4.30, and do not as a rule look at them until to-morrow at breakfast time. But in these exciting times, with Colonel Marchand crossing the Sahara and hoisting the French flag in a position which Kitchener of Khartoum has stated to be the key-point of the British Empire in Africa and consequently on the road to India. . . . And the French with their extraordinary .75 quick-firer field gun. . . . It all turns on what the Germans will do, the Russians having their hands full in the Far East. . . .

It was like that, when we were not discussing the desirability of the word *bleu-foncé* as an adjective to apply to cabbages in a field, or when we were not moved to queer enthusiasms over the use of words by Christina Rossetti. . . . But if you tell me that I cannot put in Tommy and drive through the rain to the candle-lit Pent—no *Eau, Gaz, Electricité* in *that* gentleman's residence—well, if you tell me that, I suppose you are right. . . . "*C'est le mur d'un silence eternel qui descend devant vous, mon vieux!*" . . . For the feeling, through a large part of a century, was for the writer very strong that Conrad was there, who *might* be consulted about a difficulty—in politics, in the architecture of a story, over an English word, or about the French for Romance—for which there is no French!

The irresistible feeling that one had about him was that he was practical, that the last thing that he was was Slav. For the Slav, to be true Slav,

must be as helpless before the vicissitudes of this
world — as helpless as is a new-born kitten, a
greyish, sprawling object, mostly jelly. A sort of
Dostoievsky! If you asked Conrad how to cir-
cumvent a banker he would have an expedient.
If you asked him whether women ought to have
a vote he would say, No! with decision. And
then, remembering the part played by women in
keeping alive the national feeling of his country,
Poland, where all the men took to drunkenness
or lechery or listnessness after the abortive revolution of 1862, he would say that the only creature
that ought to be paid the compliment of having a
vote, a thing always useless, was such a woman as
his mother, Mme. Korzeniowski, or his aunt,
Mme. Paradowski. Or any other woman! But,
as his private expedient, he said to women in
the words of the Mohammedan ranee of Palembang, "Why should you strive for domination
during the day? . . . Your power is of the night,
during which, with a whisper, you shall destroy
empires!"

— * —

The dominant attraction of Conrad's mind was
the firmness with which he held ideas after he had
contemplated a sufficient number of facts or documents. He had had great experience of the life
of normal men; his reading had been amazingly

wide and his memory was amazingly retentive. Amazingly, even to the writer, whose memory is sufficiently retentive and whose reading wide if desultory. Yet Conrad never presented any appearance of being a bookish, or even a reading man. He might have been anything else; you could have taken fifty guesses at his occupation, from, precisely, ship's captain to, say, financier, but poet or even student would never have been among them and he would have passed without observation in any crowd. He was frequently taken for a horse fancier. He liked that.

His ambition was to be taken for—to be!—an English country gentleman of the time of Lord Palmerston. There might have been worse ambitions. To understand how a Pole, born in the Government of Kiev, infinitely far from even the sea, should have desired to be that—and should have desired it with passion—the reader must keep in mind two things if not three, one of them a vivid picture in the mind of the writer. During the last century, if you went down to Tilbury Dock, you would see families of Jewish-Poland emigrants landing. As soon as they landed they fell on their hands and knees and kissed the soil of the land of freedom. For Conrad there was another side. As a child he lived in a great house

in Poland: a great house with wide avenues and
many lights at night.   One night all the lights
went out, the avenues were deserted; a sledge
without bells came before the portico.   A figure,
cloaked and muffled to the hat rim, came up the
steps and was closeted for long with the master
of the house.   Then drove away over the snow.
Conrad said he could imagine that he heard the
voice of *l'or de la perfide Albion* jingling in great
bags as the sledge went away.

For this was the emissary of Lord Palmerston,
sowing gold all over Poland so that the Polish
revolutionary spirit might be kept alive and Russia embarrassed in her encroachments on Pera or
Afghanistan.

For that was England of Conrad's early vision:
an immense power standing for liberty and hospi-
tality for refugees; vigilant over a pax Britannica
that embraced the world.   With an all-powerful
navy she had an all-powerful purse.   She was
stable, reasonable, disciplined, her hierarchies
standing in their orders, her classes settled, her
services capable and instinct with an adequate
tradition.   And ready to face Russia with fleet
or purse when or wherever they should meet.
The first English music-hall song that Conrad
heard was:

We don't want to fight but, by Jingo, if we do,
We've got the ships, we've got the men, we've got the money too.
We've fought the bear before and so we will again,
The Russians shall not have Constantinople. . . .

A Pole of last century—and above all things Conrad was a Pole of last century—could ask nothing better.

—*—

And, above all things else, as the writer has somewhere pointed out, Conrad was a politician. He loved the contemplation of humanity pulling away at the tangled skeins of parties or of alliances. Until, suddenly, a strand gave, a position cleared up, a ministry was solidly formed, a dynasty emerged. He was, that is to say, a student of politics, without prescription, without dogma, and, as a Papist, with a profound disbelief in the perfectibility of human institutions. The writer never saw Conrad read any book of memoirs except those of Maxime Ducamp and the Correspondence of Flaubert; those we read daily together over a space of years. But somewhere in the past Conrad had read every imaginable and unimaginable volume of politician's memoirs, Mme. de Campan, the Duc d'Audiffret Pasquier, Benjamin Constant, Karoline Bauer, Sir Horace Rumbold, Napoleon the Great, Napoleon III,

Benjamin Franklin, Assheton Smith, Pitt, Chatham, Palmerston, Parnell, the late Queen Victoria, Dilke, Morley. . . . There was no memoir of all these that he had missed or forgotten — down to "Il Principe" or the letters of Thomas Cromwell. He could suddenly produce an incident from the life of Lord Shaftesbury and work it into "Nostromo", which was the political history of an imagined South American Republic. That was one of the secrets of his greatness.

—*—

But certainly he had no prescription. Revolutions were to him always anathema since, he was accustomed to declare, *all* revolutions always have been, always must be, nothing more in the end than palace intrigues — intrigues either for power within, or for the occupancy of, a palace. The journalist's bar in the palace of the Luxemburg, where sits the present Senate of the Third Republic, was once the bedchamber of Marie de Medicis.

That is not to say that Conrad actively desired the restoration of the Bourbons; he would have preferred the journalists to remain where they were rather than have any revolution at all. All revolutions are an interruption of the processes of thought and of the discovery of a New Form . . . for the novel.

Indeed, almost the only revolution that he contemplated with enthusiasm was one by which a successful adventurer seized the reins of power. Anywhere! Some King Tom! It was not that his visions were Napoleonic. His favourite modern ruler was Louis Napoleon, Napoleon I being too big, too rhetorical, too portentous for any intimacy. We planned for many years, and even wrote one scene of, a historical novel dealing with First Empire figures. But the First Empire was gone; the subject was the attempts made to save Ney from execution; the chapter showed Louis XVIII a bewildered figure, forced to sleep and receive petitioners in a corridor between two doors, the Protocol providing lavish rooms for innumerable peers of France, lackeys and parasites, but none at all for God's anointed whose handkerchief was always dangling halfway out of his hip pocket. That was how we — or rather how Conrad, for the writer never had any political views of any strength at all — regarded restored Legitimacy. Yet he was fit to throw the teacups into the fire if you derided the doctrine of the divine right of kings.

—☛—

No, on the whole, his favourite political character was Louis Napoleon as Adventurer, and even Napoleon III, Emperor of the French, roused some of his admiration. He liked gilt Third Empire furniture, all other gilding, reviews, uniforms, la Montijo, mirrors, fraudulent financiers, the Duc de Morny, the Mexican adventurer. He liked the mournful, cynical sovereign surrounded by the crowd of adventurers, *escrocs, rastacouères* and prostitutes in high places that brought down the Empire. He admired Napoleon III for his dream of a Latin Union, which Conrad found practicable and to be desired. That was probably his idea of humanity, a realm in which the solitary, cynical, not impracticable dreamer is brought down by his womankind, his relations, his servants, his hangers-on, his household. He saw the same microcosm in the bankruptcy and ruin of a Court perfumer — or of the captain of a coastwise trading ship. He prized fidelity, especially to adventurers, above all human virtues and saw very little of it in this world.

—*—

His favourite political anecdote, that which he repeated the most often, was of the Maire of the XIIIth Arrondissement who sent to Morny, then his half-brother's Minister and taking the waters at Spa, a telegram to the effect that the whole 'Rue de la Glacière was in a state of insurrection. It ended, "Que faire?" And Morny replied. . . .

But we are writing for Anglo-Saxons. This not
very edifying anecdote was Conrad's favourite but
it is not to be taken as implying that Conrad's
mind was unedified. It simply showed his contempt for the way in which human affairs are
conducted. It was as if he said, "All politicians
are such fools that you might as well conduct the
high businesses of state in the spirit of Morny.
You will only find Maires of the XIIIth Arrondissement to carry out your orders."

He desired a stable world in which you could
think and develop the New Form. And because
at no phase of the world's history has there seemed
to be a portion of the world more stable than was
England under the ruling classes of Lord Palmerston's time, he desired to be of the type of a
member of the ruling classes of England in Lord
Palmerston's day. He lived as such, and as such
he died. We are so far from those days; it seems
hardly likely that any one's withers will be wrung
if we say that he might have had a meaner ideal.

We come thus to Captain Marryatt. It would
be too much to say that Marryatt had any influence at all on Conrad as writer — though Conrad
was of opinion that Marryatt had profoundly in-
fluenced his writing — but the effect of Marryatt

on Conrad as philosopher *tel quel*, and as English gentleman, could not be too much stated. Indeed, in the course of our last meeting, the writer reminded Conrad that almost the first literary opinion Conrad ever uttered at the Pent was in eulogy of Marryatt. Conrad replied that he remained exactly of that opinion: Marryatt was, after Shakespeare, the greatest novelist as delineator of character, that England has produced. The opinion must be limited to what it covers, and that strictly. Conrad was not saying that Marryatt was, say, nearly as great a poet as Shakespeare; he was saying that Marryatt observed English character with exactitude and rendered it without exaggeration, all other English novelists getting their effects by more or less of caricature.

⁂

The books of the author of "Midshipman Easy" are so relegated to oblivion, being considered as boys' books, that this pronouncement may appear strange. It may, however, be recommended to the reader's serious attention as the measured opinion of no mean critic. What we are about at the moment is considering the effect of Marryatt upon the character and psychology of Conrad.

⁂

That influence at least was profound and lifelong, like the undertone of a song. During all the

years of our collaboration it was always as if Conrad were saying, "Ah: but wait till I get to my
Napoleonic novel, with the frigates in the Mediterranean." That was the golden age for such
English as are held by the sea. And during those
years we planned rather elaborately a collaboration set in late Napoleonic to Restoration days, the
central figures being Ney, and an English *milor*
with the spleen, but the narrator a frigate-lieu-
tenant, protégé of the *milor* who, coming from the
Mediterranean and gallant service with the frigates, should introduce — the Marryatt touch! . . .
We spent a great deal of time over memoirs of the
period, the writer occupying himself with Dundonald, English *milors* and the part taken by the
Tsar in the execution of Ney, Conrad getting his
information as to the Restoration period in a way
that was rather mysterious to the writer, so did
Conrad seem to have all those figures in his
mind. . . .

—*—

We discussed this novel till very late indeed in
our association. On an occasion in July, 1916,
Conrad said to the writer, "Well, you'll be able
to bring something back for the Ney book, about
campaigning in France," as we shook hands. . . .
Alas! that which wiped out so many little villages
under our eyes wiped out that book too, the writer

abandoning for many years all idea of writing—
losing indeed all ability to write. And Conrad
continued alone. . . . Thus, in "The Rover", in
the offing, you have the vigilant and capable frigate
captain! . . . And on the day of his death Conrad
was occupied—with Napoleon at Elba and the
frigate service of the Mediterranean, seeking to
live again the glamour that the English sea-
novelist had cast over his young years in Poland.
So tenacious are the glamours of our youth!

Yes! *That* influence at least was profound.
He looked at the world of human affairs with the
eyes of Jack Easy and affronted difficulties with
the coolness of Percival Keene. At that statement the reader should not smile. The tradition
of the frigate service of Dundonald and the rest
was no mean one; its influence on the British
character was far-reaching, was all-important.
And the achievement and tradition of England
during the last century cannot be ignored by those
who can be interested in the achievements and
traditions of mankind.

The writer has said too much in other places
of the influence of Marryatt on the writer himself and on Conrad to go picturesquely once more
over the matter. But there are those who have

read neither Marryatt nor the writer. Marryatt concerned himself mainly, then, with the frigate warfare of Napoleonic times. And the frigate warfare of Napoleonic times was, compared with the line of battle warfare for which stand the names of Nelson and his great captains, as something obscure, anonymous, desperate and very gallant. For thousands who shall know the names of Nelson, Howe, or St. Vincent there will be hardly one that has heard tell of Cochrane. Yet this little service was incessant, pursued under desperate conditions of weather and of inshore work, the frigates being only upon occasion the mere eyes of the fleet, the great fleets with the great first-raters rolling majestically from ocean to ocean, half the world over and then back again to fight now and then a Trafalgar or an Aboukir. But the frigates were at it every day in the Mediterranean.

—*—

Such a service, without comfort, without advertisement, almost without the glory of the King's uniform, for its officers dressed like sweeps, remained midshipmen to the age of forty and were betallowed to the elbow — was the meaning of England to Conrad, as to the writer during his younger years. One saw the self-sacrifice, the patience, the fidelity. And if Conrad in later

years wrote of fidelity as the key-word of his
"message", it was of this fidelity that he was
thinking. Of fidelity not to a realm from which
they were for so long absent, and not to a royal
countenance which never shone upon them, but
of fidelity to an idea, to a service.

The idea was this: In the first place came the
sea, the sea not as a bitter element, but as an in-
strument by means of which the frigates battled
against inefficiency, strange customs, the eating of
frogs, wooden shoes. Upon the sea were only
the English — and the French; the English as the
representatives of that Almighty which holds the
sea in the hollow of His hand, the English, blond,
hardy, cunning, vigilant, each one six foot and
over, jolly, in the exact image of their Maker,
cordial. The French, the subordinates, representatives of Satan, perpetually driven off the sea
to hide behind the moles of Toulon or of Cher-
bourg, perpetually creeping out as do bedbugs
from crevices in walls. . . . One Englishman was
worth one, three, seventeen, twenty-seven French-
men. . . . There was the sea, then, and that its
business, its function.

Presumably the frigates did succeed in their
work, though if you read French textbooks you

would hardly think so, any more than when reading the Americans you will hear much about
the *Shannon* and the *Chesapeake*. According to the
French it was *l'or de la perfide Albion* that did the
trick. In that way Conrad got it both ways, since
he liked a nation that had both its sea service and
its gold. Gold also is sterling, incorruptible, and
has its fidelities. In the meantime, there had
grown up another service with a tradition almost
identical — that of the British mercantile marine,
of ships not too vast to be impermeable to the
weather, making, by means of the caprices and
brutalities of the winds, engrossed and perpetual
departures and landfalls round dangerous head-
lands. Nowadays you will find little enough difference between the coastwise men of any nation
but in the seventies and eighties of last century
Conrad, by dint of experience, found in that service, muted but almost more patient and engrossed,
the tradition of Marryatt's frigates. It was fidelity
to an ideal, the ideal of the British merchant service; it was still more a tradition working efficiently.
For in that service, all going to make up the record of British-owned bottoms, even if they sailed
under the flag of Siam, all going to contribute to
the long story of what is the shipshape, are hundreds of Dagoes, Lascars, Swedes, Danes, Finns,
Negroes, Americans, Kruboys. . . . And one Pole.

Conrad then, in his misty youth that seemed
to pass in great houses or in the prison yards of
the exiled child, and mostly at night or at night-
fall, read with engrossment Marryatt and Fenimore Cooper, and so sowed the seeds of his
devotion to England. He had his devotion to his
art and his devotion to his second country. In
the end his devotion to his second country over-
came his devotion to his art. The only occasion
on which the writer ever questioned the actions
of Conrad — and it is the truth that this was the
only occasion on which any action of Conrad's
known to the writer was ever even questionable!
— was when that writer accepted membership of
the British Academy. This as a writer he should
not have done, nor as an artist. The body was
without venerability, committed to courses of
propaganda, and of a habit, to be destructive to
the art by which Conrad had made his name, to
which he owed fidelity.

—*—

Accordingly on a given occasion the writer remonstrated against this questionable action. It
was during sad times for the nation, in a gloomy
room of the most architecturally lugubrious build-
ings that are to be found near the Marble Arch
in London. Conrad was depressed; there was no
one that was then not depressed. The writer, the

occasion being one for clearings-up of everything
that could be cleared up, put the question as to
why Conrad had, how Conrad could have, thus
denied the gods of his manhood. A knighthood
yes! Any sort of Order, yes! A C.B.; an O.B.E.!
... It had not been ten years or much more since,
when talking of the possibilities of such a founda-
tion, Conrad had said that were he offered its
insignia he would wear them on the seat of his
trousers — a gibe which we immediately introduced into "The Inheritors."

—*—

The reader should understand that this matter
is one which divides forever — into sheep and
goats — the world of the arts. There are some few
artists who will accept Academic honours; to the
majority of those who are really artists the idea
is abhorrent, and those who accept such honours
betray their brothers. To this majority Conrad
had enthusiastically belonged. You had Flaubert
who refused, you had Zola who all his life sought,
academic distinction. For Conrad there had used
to be no question as to which to follow. Now he
had followed Zola.

—*—

Conrad answered with mildness. And nothing
could have been more unlike Conrad. Both of
us being upholders of the duel, we had always

lived together under a sort of standard of for-
mality. Except upon Belgian railways when Conrad would refuse with fire to show his ticket to
collectors because he was an Englishman and they
some sort of Dagoes, the writer never remembers
otherwise to have remonstrated with the author
of "Heart of Darkness." . . . But Conrad answered with heavy and depressed mildness. . . .
Yes, to have accepted that honour might have the
aspect of denying the gods of his youth. That
was a thing to be regarded with depression. On
the other hand England had offered him hospital-
ity; he had been granted fame in England and the
opportunity to live in Kent where the lines of the
fields run quietly one into the other. England was
desirous of founding an institution that should, as
a part of its functions, do some sort of honour to
the trade of authorship. The company in which
he found himself, admirable as it was, was not
exactly that which could have been expected. But,
if it was a question of his private principles as
against any honour he could show the English
State, his private principles must go by the board.

It was a point of view.

V

The most English of the English, Conrad was the most South French of the South French. He was born in Beaucaire, beside the Rhône; read Marryatt in the shadow of the castle of the good king Réné, Daudet on the Cannebière of Marseilles, Gautier in the tufts of lavender and rosemary of the little forests between Marseilles and Toulon, Maupassant on the French torpedo boats on which he served and Flaubert on the French flagship, *Ville d'Ompteda*. With the Sabran-Penthievres and other Macmahonists he painted red the port of Marseilles, intrigued for Napoleon III, hired, since there was nothing else to be hired, an unpainted four-in-hand from a coachbuilder's yard and drove, buried in actresses and the opera chorus, to the races. So he made the French navy too hot to hold him. That, however, is also the spirit of the traditional British navy. The writer is never tired of reciting the terms of the offence for which his great-uncle, Tristram Madox, was cashiered: in that, whilst drunk, he swam ashore from the flagship without leave and riotously assaulted Mr. Peter Parker of Valetta, tobacconist.

The one offence is more French, the other more
English. . . .

—✹—

As above, however, Conrad again and again
recounted his Marseilles exploit. No doubt with
the fall of Macmahon and the disappearance of
any hope for the Bonapartists the chance of a
career for Conrad in the French navy so diminished as to leave that service with few attractions.
Conrad's influence and *attachés* in France were
all Third Empire. He would relate the instance
of the unvarnished coach with great energy and
fire and then, dropping his hands with mock
senility, exclaim, "Alas, *tel que vous me voyez.*
. . . Now I am an extinct volcano. . . ."

—✹—

It was not, however, that. It was merely that
diminished circumstances had reduced the team
of four to the old mare or some *remplacant*. We
would drive down to Hythe or hire a motor that
broke down eight times in eighteen miles and go
between the shallow downs up the Elham valley —
at the top of which he died — to Canterbury. And
at once Conrad was the sailor ashore. He *had*
to find a bar and have a drink, the writer, with the
prudishness of the Englishman in his own county,
waiting outside. For you must not have a drink
in the bar of your own county town. A lunch at

the farmer's ordinary with five pints of beer; tea in the smoking room with whiskies brought in on the tray! But in the bar, never! The point is a fine one. But Conrad, though at home he was the English country gentleman and other things permitting, would have bred shorthorns and worn leggings, threw, in his Jack-ashore frame of mind, these considerations to the wind. A drink in the bar was provided for in King's Regulations. You might not be thirsty: it had to be.

—*—

Conrad's biography as narrated in those days to, and in presence of, the writer, might as well here come in. . . . We have arrived, at any rate in the writer's mind, at about the time when we dropped, ostensibly for good, any hope of bringing "Romance" to a finish and took to collaborating on "The Inheritors." By that date the writer had heard enough of Conrad's autobiography, sufficiently repeated, to have a rounded image of his past—such an image at any rate as Conrad desired to convey. For, like every inspired raconteur Conrad modified his stories subtly, so as to get in sympathy with his listener. He did it not so much with modifications of fact as with gestures of the hand, droppings of the voice, droopings of the eyelid and letting fall his monocle—and of course with some modifications of the facts. So the story, afterwards used in " A Smile of Fortune ", told to the writer alone was one thing and told to his sprightly, very intelligent aunt, Mme. Paradowski, was something quite different. It would be thinner, less underlined, more of a business-like subject for treatment if told to the writer alone; when told to the French lady — who was also a novelist — it would be much livelier, much more punctuated with gestures and laughs — much more *pimenté*, in fact, the story of a sailor's *bonne fortune*.

It was the only story of a *bonne fortune* that the writer ever heard told by Conrad. And the note may as well here be made that in all our extreme intimacy, lasting for many years, neither of us ever told what is called a smoking-room story. We never even discussed the relations of the sexes.

So, at the turn of the century — for "The Inheritors" must have been published about 1901 and, having been written rather fast, must have been begun in 1900 — the history of Conrad appeared much as follows to the writer. He was born — not, of course, physically in Beaucaire, but in that part of Poland which lay within the government of Kiev — in Ukrainia, in the Black Lands where the soil is very fertile. He was born

around 1858. At any rate he was old enough to
remember the effects of the Polish Revolution of
the early sixties—say 1862. The oldest—the
first—memory of his life was of being in a prison
yard on the road to the Russian exile station of the
Wologda. "The Kossacks of the escort," these
are Conrad's exact words repeated over and over
again, "were riding slowly up and down under
the snowflakes that fell on women in furs and
women in rags. The Russians had put the men
into barracks, the windows of which were tallowed. They fed them on red herrings and gave
them no water to drink. My father was among
them."

—✳—

(The implication is of course that Conrad's
father died of thirst behind those windows that
were tallowed so that the men should not look
out and see their womenfolk. Actually, of course,
Conrad's father did not die in these circumstances,
but it was not until quite lately that the writer was
aware of his misapprehension. . . . This, however, is the exact history of a relationship.)

—✳—

Conrad remained with his mother in exile until
he was nine or ten, then, his mother being threat-
ened with an immediate death from tuberculosis,
they were allowed to return to Poland. Conrad's

mother was a woman of great beauty of physique and of character. Her face was oval, her black hair braided round it, her eyes intent, her manner quiet but spirited. His father was less effectual, the prime mover of an abortive revolution, a fact which Conrad deprecated. His father was not so dark as his mother; untidy, bearded, with high cheek bones, he was the proprietor, not professionally but as a revolutionist, of a famous newspaper in which he wrote a great deal. He was constantly writing: his style was not very distinguished.

Of his father Conrad spoke always deprecatorily. This was partly politeness. Whoever you were, his interlocutor, all that pertained to you—your father and all your ancestors—must be superior to his. It was his poor little books, his poor little brains, his poor little exploits set against all your splendours. Partly, too, it really pained him to think that his father had been a revolutionary—and an unsuccessful revolutionary at that; as if he had been prenatally connected with something not shipshape! For his mother he had on the other hand that passionate adoration that is felt by the inhabitants of Latin and Western Slav countries for their mothers and that seems so "foreign" to the Anglo-Saxon. Oddly but comprehensibly, when he spoke of his mother as revolutionary he was full of enthusiasm. For him the Polish national spirit had been kept alive by such women as his mother: the men were hopeless. Again not shipshape. This was not difficult to understand. The men were prohibited from living a life of their own. The only career that the Russians allowed them to study for was that of the law. So they were all either lawyers or babblers — or both — and without any practical training. This for generations and generations. . . .

--*--

As for class — the Korzeniowskis were country gentlemen, for all the world like an English County Family, with land lived on and owned since the darkest ages, untitled, but aristocrats to the backbone; what is called in England "Good people", a term which is untranslatable into any other language and incomprehensible even to Americans. This made Conrad feel at home in Kent; many times he said so. The feudal spirit survived in the territories of the great landowners.

--*--

Conrad had an uncle — Paradowski — who was a great Pan, guardian to the children of half the noble families of that Government. He had a longish — as if squared — face, a long nose, meditative hands that were always pausing in some action and long brownish hair that fell rather Germanly

over the collar of a velvet coat. It was to his
great country house that the emissary of Palmerston had come. (The writer's friend Count
Potocki tells the writer that the name of this uncle
must have been Bibrowski. The name Paradowski
remains, however, very firmly in the writer's mind.
Conrad was inordinately proud and fond of this
uncle and fully four fifths of his conversation
when it referred to his Polish days concerned
itself with this relative: there were, for instance,
the Paradowski dragoons, a famous Russian regiment named after him or his ancestors. Similarly
in early days Conrad always wrote and pronounced
his patronymic as "Kurzeniowski"; the correct
transliteration would appear to be "Korzeniowski." It does not seem to matter much.)

This uncle stood well with the Russians. Before that abortive revolution he had been a close
friend of one of the Grand Dukes and had had
a part in drafting the constitution that the Czar
had proposed to grant to Poland. In the revolution he had taken no part, not because he was
indifferent to the interests of Poland but because
he knew it must prove abortive and cause much
suffering and persecution to the Russian Poles.
Besides, it brought about the rescinding of the
constitution. After the revolution he busied him-

self with alleviating the sufferings of his compatriots; he fed legions of the starving dispossessed; he secured the return of their patrimonies to the children of the exiled. Amongst these last was Conrad: his uncle secured the return to him of half the great confiscated estate of his father and got him permission to reside in Russian Poland, in his own great house. (The emissary of Palmerston had by the by been sent away with a flea in his ear.)

—✳—

Here for years and years Conrad read Marryatt —and Fenimore Cooper. And it was one of the little ingenuous pleasures of Conrad to remember that in Paris after Waterloo, as recorded in the Memoirs, more crowds followed Sir Walter Scott and Fenimore Cooper on the boulevards than ever followed the King of Prussia. It pleased him to find one of his early heroes thus blessed by Fame of the bronze lungs. To this information the writer added the other that in that same Paris of that same date Assheton Smith, the *milor* of incredible wealth and *spleen* was, according to the journals, followed about by crowds even greater than attached themselves to the Czar of Russia. Out of a sort of tacit politeness we never tried to decide whether the King of Prussia or the Czar of Russia had the larger following. But Assheton

Smith was to have been the central figure of our novel about the execution of Ney—the *milor* with the spleen intervening nearly successfully to save the *beau sabreur*. This, not because he felt any sympathy for Ney but because he desired to put a spoke in the wheel of Wellington and Blücher and all the fighting fellows who were beginning to think themselves of much too much importance, though merely younger sons. However, he made too much progress in the affections of the Czar's Egeria, so Ney was shot by the Czar's orders, just opposite the Closerie des Lilas on a spot occupied now by a station of the Seaux Railway . . . to spite Assheton Smith.

The writer never understood why it was always night in Poland; so, however, it remains for him: a long white house, in the dark, with silver beeches in an avenue or, ghostly, in groups. Indoors was Conrad, right through adolescence, forever reading in the candlelight of an immense, stately library, with busts on white plinths and alternate groups of statuary in bronze. His uncle would be in a rather subterranean study at the other end of the vast house—writing his memoirs. When these two ever met the writer never knew; of meals or even of bed he heard nothing; it was a perpetual reading. As for the uncle's memoirs. . . . Years after, not so long ago, the writer found Conrad in a state of extreme perturbation. He said, "My dear faller, you must go with me to Boulogne! You'll have to fight the second, of course. It's always done in Polish duelling!" It is part of what gives vagueness to this narrative that Conrad always credited the writer with an almost supernatural prescience as to his, Conrad's, most remote or most immediate past. He would say, "You remember when I was on the *Flower of Surabaya*, old Corvin, the supercargo, had that shaving set that I lost on the *Duke of Sutherland* . . ." naming two ships and a supercargo of whom the writer had never yet heard. . . . So on this occasion the writer naturally agreed to go to Boulogne and pictured an immense, black moustached opponent in a busby, a frogged dolman, top boots and a cavalry sabre whose bare blade he caressed with his left hand. . . . And it was not for several days, during which we made preparations for the journey, that the reason for our journey itself was made clear to the writer. Conrad was too distressed to talk about it.

It appeared that the uncle Paradowski, almost viceroy of Russian Poland and guardian to half the sons and daughters of the Polish nobility of his province, had had unheard-of opportunities of learning all the matrimonial and family scandals of his neighbours. All these he had set down in his journal — and this journal had just been published. It had caused the wildest consternation in Poland and as Conrad was the legal heir of M. Paradowski the responsibility for the publication was considered to be his. The son of one of the most horribly aspersed couples had therefore challenged Conrad and was coming to Boulogne. Conrad was horrified to the point of madness; and he was justified. That poor fellow shot himself in despair over the revelations, in the railway carriage, on the journey. So we never fought. . . .

Conrad emerges then from the glamourous shadows of Poland, making the Grand Tour with a lively young tutor. For the first time, in Venice, from a window, he saw in the Giudecca a ship — a British schooner.

As to biography during the next few years the writer becomes hazy. Conrad himself perhaps wished to throw a haze over a part of his life that was for him a period of indecisions. At one time he would say that he had determined to go to sea, years before, when first reading Marryatt; at another, that a blaze of desire sprang up in him on

sight of that British schooner with the emotional
lines of her hull; at one time that he rushed back
to Poland to communicate his decision to his uncle;
at another that he finished the Grand Tour on the
conventional lines, but arguing with his tutor and
at last finally breaking very gradually the news to
his uncle. His uncle thought him mad; there need
be no doubt about that; no Pole had ever gone to
sea; all Poles had always been lawyers; Conrad
must not go to sea but must study for the law. At
the university of — was it? — Lemberg.

Conrad at any rate went to Marseilles, and
entered the French navy. By the influence of his
uncle — the Poles have always had great influence
in the chancelleries and ministries of Europe —
he was granted a commission in that service. In
it he remained an indefinite time, leaving with the
rank — he was specific as to that — of *Lieutenant
de Torpilleurs de la Marine Militaire Française*.
During that time, on the French flagship *Ville
d'Ompteda*, he had witnessed the bombardment of
a South American town. The town comes back to
the writer as Caracas; but apparently Caracas is inland, so the flagship can hardly have bombarded it.
Perhaps Conrad went with a landing party inland
to that capital. In that way he saw the landscape
of the track to the silver mine of "Nostromo."

There followed the period of sailor-ashorishness in Marseilles with the Bonapartist aristocracy. After the episode of the unvarnished coach loaded with actresses Conrad telegraphed to his uncle to come and pay his debt and embarked on his Carlist adventure. This is told sufficiently, as Conrad used to tell it by word of mouth, in the episode of the *Tremolino* in "The Mirror of the Sea." When taking this episode down from Conrad's dictation — as indeed when taking others of his personal recollections down from dictation at times when Conrad was too crippled by gout and too depressed to write — the writer noticed that Conrad sensibly modified aspects and facts of his word-of-mouth narrations. The outlines remained much the same, the details would differ.

As told by Conrad — and the writer must have heard all Conrad's stories five times and his favourite ones much more often — the Carlist adventure was as follows: At the date of his leaving the French service the Carlist War was being desultorily waged in the North of Spain. (The Carlists were the supporters of Don Carlos, the legitimist Pretender to the Spanish throne.) The cause of the Carlists sufficiently appealed to Conrad; it was Legitimist; it was picturesque and carried on with at least some little efficiency. It offered a chance of adventure. In company with like-minded friends, then, Conrad set to work at providing rifles for the army of the Pretender. They purchased a small, fast sailing ship — the *Tremolino*, beautiful name. And of all the craft on which Conrad sailed this was the most beloved by him. In our early days her name was seldom off his tongue and, when he mentioned her, his face lit up. Nay, it lit up before he mentioned her, the smile coming, before the name, to his lips.

—*—

The writer never heard, in those days, what make of ship she was. He was expected to know that. Conrad would say, "You know how the *Tremolino* used to come round. . . ." So the writer imagined her as a felucca, with high, bowed, white sails against storm clouds and rust-coloured cliffs. She was the beautiful ship — as Turgenev was the beautiful Russian genius.

—*—

Pacing up and down Conrad would relate how they ran those rifles. The method was this: They would load the *Tremolino*, at Marseilles, with oranges, bound ostensibly for Bordeaux or any up-channel port. Thus, "If any Spanish gun-boat accosted us we would have a perfectly good bill of lading. Out in the Channel we would meet a British schooner and throwing the oranges overboard we would load up with rifles. . . ." Those particular sentences, with their slightly unusual use of the word "would", Conrad never varied. . . . He would have begun his story, unemotionally, with such historic explanations as his hearer seemed to need. Then he would come to the *Tremolino* and his face would light up. This emotion would last him for a minute or two. At, as it were, the angle where Spain turns down from France in the Mediterranean, as if the *Tremolino* had got thus far and was just going through the blue water with her burden of oranges, he would render his voice dry to say either, "The method was this. . . ." Or, "Our modus operandi was as follows. . . ." And then, after taking a breath, "Out in the Channel we. . . ." He would then go on to explain the necessities they had when making that landfall. "You could bribe any Spanish *guarda costa* on land with a few pesetas or a bottle or two of rum. . . ." But the officers of the gunboats that patrolled the coast were incorruptible. . . .

—⋆—

"So one night the landlord of the inn omitted to show the agreed-on light. He was drunk. In the morning we saw a Spanish gunboat steaming back and forth in the narrow offing. The bay was a funnel, like this. . . . We ran the *Tremolino* on a rock, set fire to her. Swam ashore and got country

clothes for a disguise and proceeded to Marseilles
as best we could. Penniless. Without a penny."

In telling these stories Conrad would thus occasionally duplicate his words, trying the effect of
them.   Then we would debate: What is the practical, literary difference between " Penniless " and
"Without a penny "? You wish to give the effect,
with the severest economy of words, that the disappearance of the *Tremolino* had ruined them, permanently, for many years. . . . Do you say then,
penniless, or *without a penny?* . . . You say *Sans
le sou:* that is fairly permanent. *Un sans le sou*
is a fellow with no money in the bank, not merely
temporarily penniless.   But "without a penny"
almost always carries with it, "in our pockets."
If we say then "without a penny", that connoting
the other, "We arrived in Marseilles without a
penny in our pockets." . . . Well, that would be
rather a joke: as if at the end of a continental tour
you had got back to town with only enough just to
pay your cab-fare home.   Then you would go to
the bank. So it had better be " penniless." That
indicates more a state than a temporary condition.
. . . Or would it be better to spend a word or two
more on the exposition? That would make the
paragraph rather long and so dull the edge of the
story. . . .

It was with these endless discussions as to the
exact incidence of words in the common spoken
language — *not* the literary language — that Conrad's stories always came over to the writer. Sometimes the story stopped and the discussion went on
all day; sometimes the discussion was shelved for
a day or two. There were words that we discussed
for years. One problem was, as has already been
hinted at: How would you translate *bleu-foncé*
as applied to a field of cattle cabbage: the large
Jersey sort, of whose stalks varnished walking
sticks are made? Or *bleu-du-roi?* And again,
what are the plurals of those adjectives in French
— as a side issue. . . . That problem we discussed
at intervals for ten years — the problem of the field
of cabbages, not of course the plurals. . . . Now
we shall never solve it. . . .

Conrad, then, again telegraphed to his uncle
to come and pay his debts. . . . The writer used
to have a great-uncle whose one expedient in life
was to take a cab. One day this gentleman, walking past Exeter Hall, met a lion. Exeter Hall in
the sixties was a menagerie. When he was asked,
"What *did* you do?" he would reply in tones of
mild disgust at the questioner's want of *savoir
faire,* "*Do?* Why I took a cab!" . . . In the
same way Conrad used to telegraph to his uncle

to pay his debts and to come to Marseilles to
do it!

—*—

He embarked in a French messageries steamer
as a hand before the mast and, as has been said,
made one voyage to Constantinople, seeing tents
on the hills above the European city. He returned to Marseilles. Perhaps his uncle had not
yet arrived to pay his debts or did so only just
after. Or perhaps he came three times to Marseilles. Conrad used occasionally to let drop that,
as the writer knew, he had run through three
fortunes in his life. At any rate the image re-
maining to the writer is that, as Conrad sailed
away, a ship's boy, in a British brig bound for
Lowestoft, Pan Paradowski stood on the edge of
the Cannebière, like a great land lion, lamenting
on the brink of the water his beloved, ugly duck-
ling of a nephew who should have become a seal.
. . . A sea lion. . . .

VI

Lowestoft has always seemed to the writer to be a queer, bleak, whitewashed little old place from which to begin the conquest of a language, a conspiracy against a literature, a career of fame that became world-wide. It used at any rate to be all that: queer, bleak, whitewashed, with flagstaffs, coast guards, high skies and northeast wind. The writer must have been there first at the age of five or six, and, by stretching a point or so and ignoring a couple of years, we used to arrive at the theory that coincidence had brought us together thus early. That cannot actually have been the case. When Conrad first heard or spoke an English word the writer cannot have been much more than three: so we may be said to have learnt grown-up English in about the same year. . . . But we used to keep a slight haze over our respective ages. Conrad was a little sensitive about his years, towards forty-five, and the writer did not then care.

—*—

Besides, Conrad liked coincidences—in our playtime. He liked to amuse himself with re-

semblances between himself and other great men
— Johnson collected orange peel and dried it; so
at one time Conrad had done. Or he would find
in memoirs accidental traits of resemblance between himself and Napoleon, Louis XVIII,
Theophile Gautier or General Gallifet. He
would look up from his book and read the passage
out with hilarious pleasure. He liked, as has been
said, to think that at one of the Chippendale desks
that we had at the Pent Christina Rossetti had
written and at another, given to the writer's father
as a wedding present, Carlyle, who was its donor.
He would say that "Heart of Darkness" was
written on the same wood as:

> Rest, rest, a perfect rest,
> Shed over brow and breast,
> Her face is towards the West,
> The peaceful land.
> She shall not see the grain
> Ripen on hill and plain,
> She shall not feel the rain
> Upon her hand. . . .

and "The End of the Tether" before the glass
bookshelves that had seen Carlyle write "The
French Revolution." It did not matter that Christina wrote most usually on the corner of her wash-
stand or that Carlyle had bought the desk at a
second-hand dealer's in the street next Tite Street,
Chelsea. It made indeed no difference that he

disliked the work of Carlyle or thought Christina the greatest master of words in verse. The lines just cited were the only English poetry that the writer ever heard Conrad quote. He had literally no ear for English verse. . . . But there "Heart of Darkness" had to have been written, and there the poem; here "The End of the Tether", and here "The French Revolution." . . . It was like building retrospective castles in Spain; it was squeezing the last drop out of the subject.

So with our coincidental careers. The coincidences had to be there for moments of elation. The writer, after our visit to Mr. Wells, happened to ask whether the great storm in which Conrad had come up the Channel for the first time had been identical with the great gale that had wrecked the *Plassy*. And immediately it had to be. It could not have been by seven years or so. But it *was*. . . . For the rest of our lives it had to be. It shall. So with Lowestoft. Conrad could bring himself to remember there a little boy with long, golden hair, a bucket and a spade, who used to march up to the young able seaman and ask him questions in an unintelligible tongue. . . . And indeed, in moments of *great* effusiveness, patting the writer on the shoulder, Conrad used to assert that it was one of the writer's books, seen on the bookstall of Geneva railway station, that had first turned his thoughts to writing English as a possibility. That *might* indeed have happened. But one detail of Conrad's narration was too much for the writer's bibliophilic prudishness—though he would connive at any time at the twisting of manageable years between two friends. But several times before the discovery of this immense coincidence Conrad had related how he had stood on the Geneva railway platform, looking at the bookstall and idly wondering what he was going to do next with his life. He had been recovering from an illness, in the same hydrotherapy as that in which Maupassant died. Another coincidence. He had seen a row of small, canary-yellow—remember the canary yellow—volumes. They were the books of the *Pseudonym Library* that Mr. Garnett had fathered—about the colour and not much larger they were than a packet of Maryland cigarettes at 1 fr. 50. But they were famous throughout Europe. There was no railway bookstall on which you did not find them. . . . And looking at them Conrad said, "Why should I not write, too?" . . . The writer's third book had been published in that very year, fathered too by Mr. Garnett, issued by the same firm in a series called the *Independent Library.* . . . It might very well have been on the bookstall, the series having been intended for foreign circulation. There was nothing to make the thing inherently even improbable. . . . Alas! The writer's work was bound in a sort of decayed liver colour: the most hideous that the writer has ever even imagined. "So it couldn't be me," as the old mare said. But nothing would have pleased Conrad's generous and effusive moods better than to claim the writer as his literary godfather. He was like that.

＊

Years later, the writer having landed in this country at Rouen, it occurred to him as his heel struck the quay: Conrad began to write "Almayer's Folly" in the stateroom of a ship moored in this very port. When he looked up from his desk, through the porthole, he used to see the inn at which Emma Bovary met her lover. Is that then this very spot? Do I then begin where Conrad began that other battle? . . . In an interval the writer asked Conrad whether these spots could be coincidental. He at once began to be very animated on a drooping occasion. "Yes, yes," he said. "Opposite the very spot. . . . Two doors to the left of the road that goes up to the Poste Centrale. . . . My dear Ford. . . . The very spot." That coincidence the writer will not attempt to disturb.

Conrad landed, then, at Lowestoft when the writer was about three, and Conrad himself not much more than twenty, the writer is fairly certain, in 1877. Here he heard his first English words, to recognise them. They were: "Eggs and bacon or marmalade?" He was sitting in the bar of a public-house he had been taken to by an old gentleman who eventually invited him to stay. Every morning at breakfast the old gentleman uttered the above morning shibboleth of England and then went to his business. He was the proprietor of the famous Lowestoft pottery works, so eventually Conrad served his time as a Boy on a brig owned by the pottery proprietor. It made fortnightly voyages to Newcastle for coal needed by the pottery. In such coastwise service he passed the time necessary for him to become by turn A.B., second mate and master. He became a naturalised British subject just before passing for master. . . .

It was during all these years that he read. Men at sea read an inordinate amount. During the watches when they are off duty they can, if they are so minded, sit about by the hour with books, engrossed, like children. A large percentage of the letters received by writers from readers come from sailors either in the King's or the merchant service. Conrad had a great many such correspondents; one of his own, a naval officer, the writer curiously shared with Conrad. As each of our books came out he would write to its author, from off Gibraltar, from the China seas, from some Pacific station—very good letters. He seemed to have no idea of any relationship between his two addressees, but as he never gave the name of a ship neither of us ever wrote to him. His letters ceased after 1914.

It was Conrad's great good luck to be spared the usual literature that attends on the upbringing of the British writer. He read such dog-eared books as are found in the professional quarters of ships' crews. He read Mrs. Henry Wood, Miss Braddon—above all Miss Braddon!—the *Family Herald*, rarely even going as high as the late William Black or the pseudo-literary writers of his day. He once or twice said that going down Ratcliffe Highway he was jumped out at from a doorway by a gentleman who presented him with a pocket copy of the English Bible. This was printed on rice paper. He used the leaves for rolling cigarettes, but before smoking always read the page. So, he said, he learned English. The writer has always imagined this story to be one of Conrad's mystifications. Normally he would express the deepest gratitude to the writers of the *Family*

Herald — a compilation of monthly novelettes, the grammar of which was very efficiently censored by its sub-editors — and above all to Miss Braddon. She wrote very good, very sound English; machined her plots inoffensively and well; was absolutely workmanlike, her best novels being the later and less-known ones. Long after this period of seamanship Conrad read "The Orange Girl", a novel placed in the time of Charles II. He recognised in it, so he then said, all the qualities that he had found in this novelist's work when he had been before the mast. Miss Braddon learned Greek at the age of eighty in order to read Homer in the original. She died only very lately.

From that time, for ten years, Conrad followed the sea. The deep sea, reading all sorts of books. Once an officer with quarters of his own he resumed his reading of French along with the English popular works. He read with the greatest veneration Flaubert and Maupassant; with less, Daudet and Gautier; with much less Pierre Loti. Tormented with the curiosity of words, even at sea, on the margins of the French books, he made notes for the translation of phrases. The writer has seen several of these old books of Conrad, notably an annotated copy of " Pecheur d'Islande " — and of course the copy of "Madame Bovary" upon the end papers and margins of which "Almayer's Folly" was begun.

—*—

Of Conrad's deep-sea life the writer proposes to say next to nothing. Intimately mixed up as he was with the writing of so many of Conrad's sea stories he could not disentangle to his own satisfaction which version of a semiautobiographic story, like "Heart of Darkness", was the printed story, which the preparation for the printed story, as Conrad told it to the writer, which the version that Conrad told for the pleasure of chance hearers and which was, as it were, the official autobiographic account. Occasionally, as in his account of his meeting with Roger Casement on the fringe of the bush outside Boma, Conrad would turn to the writer and say, "You'll keep that, *mon vieux*, for my biography, . . ." speaking semijocularly.

—*—

However, by a curious fatality, during the late war the writer happened to come across a largish body of writing in the form of letters written by Conrad from aboard ship to a compatriot. By Conrad as politician, not as seaman! It was precisely a body of writing, since each of the letters was a sort of essay on international politics, and it was curious in that it was to all intents and purposes completely uninteresting. It was in a sense passionate in that it was filled with aspirations that Great Britain should join in one combination or another against Russia. She was to join Germany, Austria, France — any one, so long only as she fought the Bear. But all these letters were written with a fluency, such that, had they come before the writer editorially, he would at once have thrown them into the waste-paper basket. It was as if Lord Macaulay had been writing leaders for a popular paper. . . . Before that one of Conrad's relatives had showed the writer a number of letters that Conrad had written to the *Indépendance Belge*. These were quite another matter — admirably written, intensely emotional. As if Pierre Loti had had some heart! They had in fact, as is to be expected, a great deal of the body and substance of "Heart of Darkness."

At both of these documents however, the writer did no more than glance. The lady had treasured up as cuttings her nephew's correspondence and, when Conrad was out of the room, presented the bundle to Conrad's *ami le poète*. He read them for perhaps half an hour before Conrad came in again; then their author exhibited so much perturbation that the writer desisted. The probability is that Conrad burned the bundle. . . . It was very similar with the other letters. They were lent to the writer by their addressee at a time when the writer was extremely occupied; he glanced at them for long enough to form the opinion expressed above and then put them away. Before he had had time to look at them again it occurred to him that Conrad might prefer him not to read them. He accordingly wrote to Conrad and received the answer that Conrad would extremely prefer that the letters should not be reread and the author returned them to their owner. It is to be hoped that they will not be disinterred.

It should not be inferred that Conrad had anything to hide. He disliked the writer's reading his early works out of the shyness that attends the maturity of every author. This writer would give a good deal if the shelf in the British Museum that contains his early writings could be burned, and Conrad would occasionally say that the idea of the writer or any one else reading certain of the stories of "The Outpost of Progress" or even certain paragraphs of his later work caused him to have *chair de poule* all down his spine. It is like a feeling of physical modesty.

However, in moments more robust he would declare that the articles in the form of letters were remarkable productions. He would remind the writer of his aunt's expressed opinion that those letters formed magnificent prose; and in moments of depression over his then work he would declare that what he had written in French before ever trying English was infinitely above anything he could do in the inexact, half-baked language that English was. He put it that the idea of really *writing* English — an English that should have an abiding value — never appeared to him practical whilst he was at sea. He would write essays and long letters with the idea of improving his vocabulary for social occasions. Then, one day, writing an imaginary letter to the *Times* about some matter professional to the British Mercantile Marine, he felt as if he had really "bitten into his pen." . . . The earlier letters at which the writer glanced sufficiently confirmed this. It was not that they were bad: they were just glib.

At what moment of writing or reading on the bridge, in what harbour Conrad thus found the religion of English prose the writer does not remember. It was probably in Sydney during a period in a convalescent home. It comes back that this is what Conrad said, but that may very well be a mistake. . . . Conrad, however, used to

say that in that convalescent home they were fed
on tomatoes and milk, a horrible combination;
occasionally also he used to say that his early work
was like tomatoes and milk taken together.   A
horrible combination! he would add. . . . Or, of
course, the revelation of his powers may have come
to him in Rouen.

Anyhow, somewhere on the dark waters Conrad found religion.

We had left Lowestoft and passed for master.
. . . We made the voyage in the *Judea, Do or
Die*—actually the *Palestine*—that you find narrated in "Youth."   In the East we passed so and
so many years.   You find the trace of them in
"The End of the Tether", to go no further outside
"The Youth" volume.   We commanded the
Congo Free State navy—for the sake of "Heart
of Darkness."   So we have the whole gamut of
youth, of fidelity and of human imbecility. . . .
And if the writer write "we"—that is how it
feels.   For it was not possible to be taken imperiously through Conrad's life, in those unchrono-
logical and burning passages of phraseology, and
not to feel—even to believe—that one had had,
oneself, that experience.   And the feeling was
heightened by Conrad's affecting to believe that

one had, at least to the extent of knowing at all times where he had been, what seen, and what performed.

The scenes of Conrad's life as afterwards rendered, say in "Heart of Darkness", are really as vivid in the writer's mind from what Conrad said as from what Conrad there wrote. It is a curious affair. Actually under the writer's eyes are the bright, lit-up keys of a typewriter. Yet perfectly definitely he sees *both* the interior and the outside of a palm-leaf hut, daylight shining through the interstices. A man lies on the floor of the hut, reaching towards a pile of condensed milk tins. The man is half in shadow — half Conrad, half the writer; too tall for Conrad; stretched out a full eight feet, trunk and arms. Outside an immense grey tide, the other shore hardly visible: a few darkish trees of irregular outline. And a man — coming. In a planter's dress: breeches, leggings, a flannel shirt, a sombrero. . . . Some time before he had lifted up the branches of the forest on the opposite shore and looked across at our hut. . . . He makes a fire and gives us some soup. . . . He comes once a fortnight. . . .

We had been at the sources of the Congo: nearly to Fashoda, says the ungeographical part

of our minds that once pored over a map of
Africa to see everywhere *Terra Incognita* — in the
eighties — and that has never again looked at a
map of Africa. We had belonged to the Humanitarian Party. The Humanitarian Party did not
approve of feeding our black troops on black
prisoners; the Conservatives did. So the Conservatives had poisoned us or something the
equivalent. And had put our quasi corpse in
charge of native bearers to take us, dead or alive,
down to Boma on the coast. It was all one to
the natives whether at Boma they delivered us
quick or dead : they were paid the same.

—✳—

Half down the Congo they had dumped us in
a hut that was a cache for condensed milk. They
had gone away for a fortnight to their own vil-
lage. . . . We extracted the condensed milk from
the tins by suction, having first pierced them with
a pocket knife. . . . The condensed milk was the
very antidote for the poison! . . . The bearers,
black, their white teeth protruding, come back,
not displeased to find us alive. Not pleased. . . .
Astonished! . . . They carried Conrad down to
Boma, a sweltering collection of tin huts. The
Bomese took great pains to keep you alive : you
must die at sea, otherwise the death rate of the
Congo Free State rises by one. . . .

At Boma then, listless from the abominable huts, we strolled out one day along the coast, between the satin sea and the steaming trees. A man, with the sunlight on his face, in white tennis shoes, with two bulldogs at his heels, stepped out of the dark forest. He said Hullo! He had strolled across Africa from the Zanzibar side in his tennis shoes, with no bearers, no escort but his bulldogs, no arms. He had such a fascination for the black fellows. That was Roger Casement. . . . There was a great deal of light, the sky blue, the sea dove-coloured and oily, the forest black-green, a wall; the beach pink; the bulldogs crashed over it to sniff at our heels. . . .

—*—

It was in pictures like that that the writer had Conrad's life, up to about the time when we en-gaged on "The Inheritors." Half of it came in a shyish way, for biography, half in pictures, the result of stray anecdotes. Thus if one or other of us happened to be nervous from overwork and we talked of nerves Conrad would say, " By Jove, after I came out of the Ospedale Italiano and went into the City to draw some pay, I was so frightened at the racket on the Underground that I had to lie down on the floor of the compartment. Nerves all to pieces. . . ." So the writer has his picture of Conrad lying between the seats on the things like duckboards that used to floor the old Underground carriages; it was only by conjunctions before and after that he pieced together that Conrad went into the Italian Hospital for Seamen in London after coming back from Boma and that from there he went to Switzerland, to the hydrotherapy near Geneva in which Maupassant died.

All to pieces as he then was he had to think of how he was going to employ the rest of his life. For following the sea he imagined that he would be no longer fit. When he was a little better he saw on the bookstall of Geneva Station those yellow volumes. The sight of them and the thought of Maupassant made him say, " By Jove! Why not write? " When he had settled that he might write he had to settle in which language his writing should be. There were French and English. In English there were no stylists — or very rare ones. French bristled with them. When he made the decision to write in English the writer does not know. He used to say that it was in Rouen harbour, opposite the hotel in which Emma Bovary had been accustomed to meet Rodolphe.

Here, looking out of his porthole across the frozen ground at the inn door, he began translating phrases from the scene between Rodolphe

and Emma at the cattle show. He said that he
began with Rodolphe's formal phrases of romantic
love that were whispered between the announce-
ments of prizes for bullocks and so, working out-
wards, reached the blanker pages of cover, title
and half-title pages. On these he began "Almayer's Folly." He was reading at the time
Daudet's "Jack" which immensely fascinated him
though he found it *trop chargé* — as who should
say, too harrowing.

What stands in the two paragraphs above Conrad told the writer over and over and over again.

In the sad years for Europe, Conrad wrote a
passage contradicting the statement made by some
one somewhere in print that he had had to choose
between writing in French or English. He stated
that from the first English had jumped at him and
held him. This was a politeness to England at
a time when extravagantly patriotic pronounce-
ments were called for from persons of foreign
origin: Henry James imagined the *beau geste* of
naturalising himself as a British subject practically
on his deathbed, Conrad this other. From the
national point of view it was desirable, from the
point of view of literary precision, to be regretted.
For it is obvious that any one who contemplates

writing and is practically bi-lingual must from
time to time hesitate as to in which language he
will write. The writer has to make the choice
every morning. He had to make the choice on
the morning after the day on which he learned
of Conrad's death. That was a choice a little more
definite than that Conrad made — but not much
more. His relations and connections in Belgium
certainly pressed him to write in French before he
even thought of writing in English. Of that the
writer was assured by Conrad's aunt, who regretted
to the last that Conrad chose to write in a language
that rendered him inaccessible to what she considered to be the civilised world. She herself
wrote several novels, notably for the *Revue des
deux Mondes*.

The point is of no great importance. Obviously if, as Conrad frequently asserted, the first
English words that he ever heard were the verses
containing the pious aspiration, "We 've fought the
Bear before, and so we will again, the Russians
shall not have Constantinople!" Those words
might well jump at a young Pole, sick to take
part in politics. What is material is that Conrad
always knew French much better than he knew
English. This only enhances the glory of his
achievements in our language. In French he was

perfectly fluent, in English never; abroad he was constantly taken for a Frenchman; no one could ever have imagined him English from his speech or bearing. Those points again are of no importance: what is miraculous is that he took English, as it were by the throat and, wrestling till the dawn, made it obedient to him as it has been obedient to few other men. The fact is extraordinary, but not incomprehensible. The writer writes French better than he does English, not because he knows French better, but precisely because he knows French worse; in English he can go gaily on exulting in his absolute command of the tongue. He can write like the late Mr. Ruskin or like the late Charles Garvice, at will. In writing, but not in speaking French, he must pause for a word; it is in pausing for a word that lies the salvation of all writers. The proof of prose is in the percentage of right words. Not the precious word; not even the startlingly real word.

—*—

We once discussed for a long time whether Conrad should write of a certain character's *oaken* resolution. As a picturesque adjective "oaken" has its attractions. You imagine a foursquare, lumpish fellow, inarticulate and apt to be mulish, but of good conscience. The writer must obviously have suggested the adjective. We turned it

down after a good deal of discussion, the writer
being against, Conrad for, its use.   Conrad liked
its picturesqueness and was always apt to be polite
to the writer's suggestions.   He could afford to
be.   We decided for "stolidity" which is more
quiet in the phrase.   Eventually the whole sentence
went. . . . The story was Conrad's "Gaspar
Ruiz."   That is a fairly exact specimen of the way
we worked during many years. . . .

Conrad then, in Rouen harbour, decided that
he would write books in English.   From that point
the following episodes come back to the writer
from Conrad's recounted autobiography.   He lay
for long in that port, because the ship upon which
he found himself as master had been seized by the
sheriff's officers, for debt.   Not of course for Conrad's debt.   The ship was one of a projected
French Rouen-to-New York line that never got
beyond that one ship, and that one ship lay there
for a long time, the financier having failed to
raise capital enough. . . . There comes in here
another rather curious coincidence between the
career of Conrad and the writer; it cannot unfortunately be narrated for the moment, one of the
parties concerned being out of reach and probably
still alive. . . . Presumably, however, if two people knock about the world in similar districts for

a number of years before acquaintanceship, they will come very near touching hands several times all unconsciously. . . .

Gradually, then, Conrad seemed to lose touch with the open sea. There opened up more and more glimpses of shore careers, so that of those relatively later days the record would seem to be one of abortive voyages. . . . Thus the writer remembers with peculiar vividness a telegram coming to Captain Conrad, telling him to assume command of a ship taking in cargo in Antwerp harbour, and a journey out in midwinter. . . . But it is only a vignette of a wintry port with icy arc lamps amongst bare trees over black water: the stowing was being done all wrong, the ship being a bad one to shift her cargo. That was apparently why Conrad had been called in. Whether she ever went to sea remains as a blank in the writer's mind.

By all accounts Conrad was a very efficient master—but extravagantly nervous about details. All the several officers who once sailed with him have narrated the same thing to the writer. Conrad would indulge in extremely dangerous manoeuvres, going about within knife-blades of deadly shores whilst his officers and crew shivered;

but over very small details of the stowing of
spars and the like he would go out of his mind
and swear the ship to pieces. In the same way,
in writing he would attack subjects almost impossible and go mad over a sentence; or, in driving,
he would shave stone posts like a madman, and then
curse the stable-boy for letting him come out with
the old instead of the new whip. . . . You get an
account of a going-about in " The Secret Sharer."
It is, however, possible that the minuteness of detail on which, according to his officers, Conrad so
insisted on board was not so very minute.

There is for instance the story of the Conway
boy. This Conrad was fond of relating as an
instance of the complete want of any sense of
responsibility in the character of the English —
or at any rate of the English when young. Conrad had then with him on a vessel in Table Bay
a third mate, or perhaps an apprentice, who had
just come from the *Conway* training ship. Bad
weather appeared to be coming on and Conrad
asked the boy if he had seen the cables properly
stowed. The boy answered that he had. The expected gale came on, blowing in-shore. It was
necessary to let go another anchor. As the cable
ran out one of its links jammed. . . . The writer
does not profess to understand this technical de-

tail. . . . The ship at any rate was in imminent danger owing to the neglect—the sheer irresponsibility—of that Conway boy. The Conway boy, at frightful risk, jumped on the cable and kicked the link into place, saving the ship. . . . Conrad used to comment that it was unimaginable that any French boy would have neglected the supervision of that cable; had he done, however, the impossible, and so neglected, he would probably not have jumped on the cable. He would have committed suicide, out of shame and knowing that his career was ended. . . . It might have been better to have jumped on the cable first, and then committed suicide. The matter under consideration was, however, responsibility. . . .

If then one of the officers who had sailed with Conrad and afterwards talked with the writer happened—as the writer strongly suspected—to have been that Conway boy it is not unlikely that he would enlarge on Conrad's hypercritical attention to detail. The people you have strafed—and Conrad said he strafed that boy until he precious nearly wanted to commit suicide—well, they take it out of you like that afterwards. That is only human nature.

At any rate Conrad, by all accounts, was a very

admirable officer.   Yet he hated the sea. . . .
Over and over again he related how overwhelming, with his small stature, he found negotiations
with heavy spars, stubborn cordage and black
weather.   He used to say, half raising his arms,
"Look at me. . . . How was I made for such
imbecilities?   Besides, my nerves were for ever
on the racket. . . ."   And he would recount how,
when he had been running up the Channel on a
moonlight night, suddenly, right under the foot of
the *Torrens*, there had appeared the ghostly sails
of a small vessel.   It was, he used to say, something
supernatural, something of the sort that was always happening at sea.   He said it wasn't so much
that his heart was in his mouth for the seconds it
took that vessel to clear; it remained in his mouth
for months after.   It was there yet when he thought
of it. . . .

On the outward voyage of the *Torrens* he had
had as a passenger Mr. Galsworthy, going to the
Cape.   They had confided in each other shyly —
each of them was writing! . . . From that sprang
up a friendship that was lifelong. . . . The bustle
that arose in the Pent when Conrad, opening a
letter, exclaimed, "Hurray . . . Jack's coming
down!"   The mare would have to go down to
Dan West's at Hythe half a dozen times that day.

. . . Once Mr. Galsworthy, arriving at Sandling Junction, found the trap too loaded. He ran beside it all the two and a half uphill miles to the Pent, talking pleasantly as he trotted. The writer has never seen anything so effortless, for Nancy went quite well, long ears and all. . . . That became one of the legendary feats of the Pent along with the writer's long shot at the rat. . . . It was the better performance. . . . It is a pity that there is no feat of Mr. Robert Bontine Cunninghame Graham's to set beside it. That mighty horseman also, with a letter announcing a visit, could wake up the studious Pent as a junction springs into life at the coming of a great mail train. . . . Conrad had very good friends.

Other departures from the sea of which Conrad liked to talk and which the writer could never chronologically disentangle were his caretaking of a warehouse on the Thames beside one of the bridges. . . . London Bridge probably . . . and his floating with Mr. Fountain Hope of a South African gold mine. . . . Why Conrad should have found the superintending of a warehouse that transshipped tinned meat attractive the writer does not know. Or perhaps he does. At any rate, Conrad talked of that time with enthusiasm as a period of fun. He had been found the job whilst waiting for a ship by a friend with a name like Krieger, with whom he afterwards lost contact. Occasionally Conrad would ask, "What's become of Krieger?" . . . They enjoyed themselves together in a jack-ashore way, going to the Royal Aquarium in the evenings or sitting on barrels in the tobacconist's shop just near Fenchurch Street Station—a great place to hear of a ship. Once when we were going to see Captain Hope—another good friend of Conrad's—at Stanford le Hope, Conrad pointed out to the writer marks that he alleged his feet had kicked in that tobacconist's counter-front. . . . No doubt other sea captains awaiting ships had borne their part.

In Fenchurch Street and particularly in the Station, Conrad was a different man—with his echoes! The gloomy light framed him very appropriately; truculences came into his voice; he knew all the bars and became at once the city-man gentleman-adventurer with an eye for a skirt that hadn't disturbed the dust that twenty years. He had to have from that tobacconist a handful of cigars—he who never smoked anything but innumerable half cigarettes from year's end to year's end, lighting up and almost immediately throwing away to light up again. There is no station like Fenchurch Street on the road to Til-

bury.   Conrad could tell you where every husky
earringed fellow with a blue, white-spotted handkerchief under his arm was going to. . . . It
most impressed the writer that in the station bar-
ber's shop was a placard that read: *Teeth scaled
two shillings, extractions sixpence.* . . . To come
home from the great waters to that!

In that mood must have been Conrad's city adventure.   It was perhaps the third fortune that he
lost.   He, Mr. Hope and a brother — Mr. Hope
may well correct the details: this is the saga told
in Fenchurch Street.   (Do you know the story of
Grunbaum who asks Klosterholm: Is it true the
story that I hear that Solomons made forty thousand dollars in St. Louis in the retail clothing trade?
Well, replies Klosterholm, the story is true, it's
the details are wrong.   It wasn't in St. Louis but in
Chicago.   It wasn't in the retail trade but in the
wholesale.   It wasn't forty thousand dollars, but
a hundred and forty thousand.   It wasn't his
money, but mine.   And he didn't make it; he lost
it.)   Conrad, then, Mr. Hope and a brother had
staked out in the South African gold fields a
claim to about a third of what is now the De
Beers Mine.   They came to London to float a
company at the time of the boom in South Afri-
cans.   Their solicitor, to begin with, with all the

deeds, was lost in the *Kinfauns Castle.* Before
they could get others the boom was on the decline;
by the time they were ready for flotation the bottom
dropped out of the market. One of the blackmailing bucket-shopkeepers, who seem indispensable as members of the British and all other
Parliaments, turned his attention to Conrad and
Company. He demanded money as the price of
a good report in his blackmailing sheet. The adventurers told him to go to hell. The prospectus
of their mine was printed by the same firm as
printed the blackmailing sheet. When the prospectus came out the little red patch on the map
that should have showed the Conrad-Hope property was well away in the territory of another
company. The blackmailer in his sheet jubilantly
pointed out that the mine must be bogus. . . .
They went nevertheless to flotation. . . .

Conrad used to describe how, having issued
their prospectus on the day of flotation, they sailed
the Thames, jubilant in a steam launch with cigars,
champagne, plovers' eggs in aspic. . . . God
knows what. They were to step ashore million-
aires. . . . They stepped ashore to find the flotation a disastrous failure. Only one hundred and
eighty — some fabulously small number — shares
had been subscribed by the public.

That was Conrad's last commercial venture. Whether he telegraphed again to his uncle he never said. . . . Let us imagine for a moment's pause what would have become of British Literature if that flotation had succeeded. . . . For Conrad was certainly a magnificent business man of the imaginative type. It might well have been Park Lane instead of the Pent. For Conrad hated writing more than he hated the sea. . . . *Le vrai métier de chien!*

Part II

EXCELLENCY, A FEW GOATS. . . .

I

WE come thus to the life purely literary.

---*---

After two and a half years we had abandoned "Romance": the problem of how to get John Kemp out of Cuba had grown too difficult. The writer's invention at any rate had failed and Conrad was too involved with his own work to do any inventing. Looking back, the period in which slowly we dragged out that preposterous series of fatalities seems one of long bush-fighting: as if we were clearing a piece of land in which the vegetation grew faster than could be dealt with by such cutting instruments as we had.

---*---

It is not to be imagined that we spent the whole of our times upon this enterprise; we each at intervals carried on work of our own. Then we would drop it, have another month's try at "Romance." Then drop that again. . . . Or sometimes one of us would write his own work in the morning; the other would write away at "Romance"; in the evenings and till far into the night we would join up. We pursued this monstrous undertaking all over the shores and near-shores of the British Channel; at the Pent, near Hythe in Kent; at Aldington; at Winchelsea in Sussex; in Bruges. . . . The most terrible struggles of all took place in a windy hotel at Knocke on the Belgian coast, with a contralto from Bayreuth practising in the basement. Her voice literally shook the flimsy house. Whilst we wrote or groaned on the fourth floor the glasses on a tray jarred together in sympathy with the contralto passages of "*Die Goetterdaemmerung.*" . . . And there was a child very ill, with only Belgian doctors; abscesses in the jaw and no dentist; gout; frigid rooms into which blew the sands from Holland; intolerable winds; interminable gusts of rain. . . . It is thus the world gets its masterpieces. Conrad was then beginning "Nostromo" in the mornings: it was going to be a slight book and very quickly finished — to make a little money.

It was, however, before that that we abandoned "Romance." We took up "The Inheritors", a queer, thin book which the writer has always regarded with an intense dislike. Or no, with hatred and dread having nothing to do with literature. What they have to do with he cannot say; some obscure nervous first cause, no doubt, that could not interest any one but a psychopathic expert.

Conrad had none of these feelings apparently. The writer's dislike for the book began as soon as the last word was written, so that he managed to shift the burden of proof-correcting—which Conrad rather liked—on to his collaborator's shoulders and from that day to this has never looked at the book. When then, during the early days of the late European struggle we met finally to settle up various matters, and when Conrad said, "As to collaborations, when it comes to our collected editions, you had better take 'The Inheritors' because it is practically all yours, and that will leave me 'Romance'—not that 'Romance' isn't practically all yours too" (Conrad talked like that!), the writer was very pleased. His intention was to suppress the book. He imagined that Conrad disliked it as much as he did himself, and was just turning it over with polite contempt. So it would never have appeared in either of our collected editions and would remain unobtainable until, with the expiration of copyright, some German research-worker might dig it up and make a pamphlet out of it.

However, a little later, Pinker, having been informed that the writer was dead or in an asylum, made in America a contract for the collected edition of Conrad, including all our collaborations

past and to come. Thus, before the writer knew
anything about it, there "The Inheritors" was,
out again, not merely in one, but in three editions.
He happened then, rather with regret, to mention
the republication to Conrad as a thing that he supposed Conrad had not been able to prevent.
Authors are forced by agents and publishers into
the republication of all sorts of works they may
wish to suppress — in the interests of a sacred
"completeness."   Conrad, however, remarked
with a great deal of feeling — with more feeling
than the writer otherwise remembers in him —
"Why not? Why not republish it? It's a good
book, is n't it? It's a *damn* good book!" And the
writer let the matter go at that — rather than imply
that Conrad would have set his name to a book
that he did not consider good, or even damn good.
He had intended to raise the matter later so as
absolutely to assure himself as to what really was
Conrad's view of this work.   But that is too late
now.   It must remain as Conrad's opinion that the
book is a *damn* good one.

—✳—

That being so we had better go on a little to
consider the exegesis of this work. . . . We had
abandoned "Romance"; the writer had just finished a preposterous work purporting to be a history of the *Cinque Ports* in elephant folio.   In

revenge it was written completely in sentences of
not more than ten syllables. The South African
War was there — or thereabouts, the writer being
an excited Pacifist whose hat was from time to
time bashed in by still more excited patriots.
Conrad was engaged with the end of "Heart of
Darkness", with thinking out "Typhoon" and
with writing "Amy Foster", a short story originally by the writer which Conrad took over and
entirely rewrote. The writer, in common with
Conrad, had a great admiration for Mr. Balfour;
the writer at least had a profound detestation for
the late Mr. Chamberlain who, off his own bat,
had caused the war. How Conrad felt towards
the late Mr. Chamberlain the writer does not remember. He was certainly more Imperialistic
than the writer. . . .

Since it may seem odd to the reader that one
author, living in close intimacy with another
author, should not know what were his friend's
views upon a point of politics so important as a
war it might be as well to say a word or two upon
how we *did* live together. Our relationships
were, then, curiously impersonal: never once did
the writer ask Conrad a question as to his past,
his ethical or religious outlook or as to any intimate point of his feelings or life. Never once

did Conrad ask the writer any such question. Never once did we discuss any political matter.

—∗—

We met at first as two English gentlemen do in a club: upon that footing we continued. We took it for granted that each *was* a gentleman, with the feelings, views of the world and composure of a member of the ruling classes of the days of Lord Palmerston — tempered of course with such eccentricities as go with the spleen of the *milor anglais.* Such eccentricities we allowed each to the other, but without question. Thus during the South African War, as has been said, the writer was an active and sometimes uproarious Pacifist. Not a pro-Boer; he would have hanged President Kruger on the same gallows as Mr. Chamberlain. Or, later, with an equal enthusiasm he supported Miss Christabel Pankhurst and the Suffragettes. Now and then on idle occasions after lunch he would declaim about either of these causes. Conrad would listen.   —∗—

From time to time, particularly whilst writing "Heart of Darkness", Conrad would declaim passionately about the gloomy imbecility and cruelty of the Belgians in the Congo Free State. Still more would he so declaim, now and then, after he had been up to London and had met Casement, who had been British Commissioner on the Congo and was passionately the champion of the natives. Then the writer would listen.

If Conrad differed from the writer he never argued, nor did the writer ever argue with Conrad. Once in his hotter youth — though he would do the same in his sober age! — the writer put his name down as willing to go with a crack-brained expedition to German Poland in order to fight the Prussians, and Conrad never so much as remonstrated, though he expressed gloomy anticipations as to what would happen to that expedition. The writer's ambition, however, was to fight the Prussians; to that Conrad offered no objection. . . .

Or, again, the writer never in his life uttered one word of personal affection towards Conrad. What his affection was or was not here appears. And Conrad never uttered one word of affection towards the writer: what his affection was or was not will never now be known. Conrad was infinitely the more lavish of praise of his collaborator's books: so lavish that at times the writer would feel like a fatuous Buddhist idol whilst Conrad went on. The writer on the other hand supposes that Conrad gathered somehow how deeply his work was admired by his companion.

Perhaps he did, perhaps he did not; that, too, will never now be known. The writer cannot remember ever to have addressed any particularly moving praise to Conrad as to his work—except in his last letter but one. . . .

—*—

It is that that makes life the queer, solitary thing that it is. You may live with another for years and years in a condition of the closest daily intimacy and never know what, at the bottom of the heart, goes on in your companion. Not really.

—*—

So there we lived, the two English gentlemen, the one bobbing stiffly to the other, like mandarins. . . . Our politics were what they were; our creeds were what they were. Out of the loyalty that is demanded of gentlemen we were both papists— but not the faintest glimmer of an idea is in the writer's mind as to what might have been the religious condition of Joseph Conrad, except that, when out driving, he would turn back rather than meet two priests. That is a Polish superstition. Once in our lives the writer addressed a remonstrance—a reproach—to Conrad. That has been already related. Once Conrad did the same to the writer.   —*—

That was very characteristic. Conrad had very strongly the idea of the Career. A career was

for him something a little sacred: any career. It
was part of his belief in the shipshape. (The
reader must not believe that, though we did not
question each other, we did not voluntarily and
at times the one to the other express our passionate
beliefs.) A career was a thing to be carried
through tidily, without mistakes, as a ship is taken
through a voyage and stowed away safely in a port.
So one day, when the writer had both started a
Review and permitted some one to make a very
indifferent play out of one of his novels that was
then being boomed by an enthusiastic Press, Conrad positively addressed a letter of serious and
formal remonstrance to the writer.

—＊—

But Conrad had certainly intensely disliked the
English Review, if not for its contents of conduct,
then for its effect on the writer's career. With a
great deal of perspicacity he pointed out that it is
ruin for any imaginative writer to edit any sort of
periodical. In the first place it is a waste of time;
in the second place it raises for you such hordes of
enemies that eventually they will bring you down
— or very nearly. All the writers you discover or
benefit will become your bitterest enemies, as soon
as your connection with a public organ ceases —
or sooner! That is human nature. Even Benjamin
Franklin observes that his eminently successful

career was made by very carefully putting himself in a position to receive — as often as not — unneeded benefits. He thus made for himself so many patrons who gave him friendly shoves on the way, whenever the opportunity occurred. And, by never conferring benefits, or by very skilfully obscuring the origin of such benefits as he did confer, he made for himself no enemies at all. . . . In addition, Conrad continued, every soul who has ever written a favourable note about you will deluge you with his manuscripts. You will be unable to print them; you will have so many thousands to call you base ingrate in private and to stone your work before the public — again, as soon as you have no organ of your own in which to revenge yourself. . . .

—*—

But even conducting a review was as nothing to the sin of allowing an indifferent play, made from one of your novels, to be produced. In that day, in England, all novelists were obsessed by the idea that if they could only get a play produced, fame, fortune and eternal tranquillity, beyond the range of all temporal griefs, would be for ever theirs. A novel *may* earn its hundreds. A play — even an unsuccessful play — will earn thousands; the receipts for a successful play run into the tens and hundreds of thousands. In addition, in England at that date there was a glamour of its own attaching to the Play. Even the Lord Chamberlain's censorship was nearly almost abolished. There was something sacred about it.

—

The writer was practically the only British novelist who did not catch that malady. It poisoned the whole of Henry James's after life; even Conrad was not immune. The writer was — and he got it in the neck, as the phrase is. There was never — there was *never* such a debacle as was that novel dramatised. It contained five acts, each of innumerable scenes; the curtain was down for twice as long as it was up; it played from 8 till 12.15. Not ten people remained till the end. The Press next day was livid with rage at the writer for daring to write a play without having studied the technique of the drama. The writer's connection with the *English Review* had just come to an end. He had had nothing to do with that play. It had been extracted from his novel by a dramatist. The writer had never even seen a rehearsal.

—

The writer did not mind; Conrad did. He minded horribly. Coming down from Town the day after he had received that letter, the writer just mentioned its reception, and left it at that. Conrad did not. He repeated the contents of the

letter all over again: the writer was ruining his
career.   The writer said that he did not care.
At that Conrad suffered really as much as he had
suffered during the reading of the first draft of
" Romance."   It was in the same department of
suffering. He sat, rather curled up in the corner
of a sofa, sick-looking and wincing, flushed, and
his eyebrows contracted downwards.

—*—

A frame of mind, a conception of life, according to which a man did not take stock of the results
of his actions upon himself, as it were at long
range, was something that he had never contemplated. As he saw life, you wrote a book, lived
circumspectly, avoided making enemies, meddled
only with what immediately concerned you; or you
passed for second mate, lived circumspectly,
avoided making enemies, concerned yourself only
with your ship and ship's company. . . . Then you
could foresee that in ten years' time, in fifteen,
in twenty, you would be promoted to the command
of the *Torrens*, the finest sailing ship afloat; to be
commodore of a great line; to be an elder brother
of the Trinity House. . . . Or the *Times* would
salute you as a great light in the literary firmament;
you would become the doyen of British letters and
an honorary member of the French Academy;
you would have a memorial service in Westminster

Abbey. Or even be buried there: an aspiration the fulfilment of which was forbidden to Nelson. . . . He desired the shipshape life.

—⋆—

That any one — *any* soul — could be indifferent to these honours was new to him, and terribly painful. He had taken it as so for granted that all proper men deserved this tranquil and as if British peacefulness! . . . In the same way in His Majesty's Army it *has* to be taken for granted that *every* officer desires promotion to the rank, eventually, of honorary Colonel commanding his regiment. Life could not otherwise go on. That any officer should be indifferent to promotion then becomes painful: as if you should not care about the dressing of the men of your unit upon inspection by the Field Marshal Commanding-in-Chief. . . . It is, in effect, the same crime as not squeezing the last drop of blood out of your subject when you are writing a book: the real crime against the Holy Ghost.

—⋆—

For *that* crime presumably is neither more nor less than to be out of harmony with the universe, and for Conrad the universe was the shipshape. Any soul wandering outside that corral in the abyss was for him a matter purely of gloomy indifference. . . . "The fellow simply does not

exist!" That was the formula. . . . That any
one with whom he was on terms of intimacy
should, all unsuspected, hold such a philosophy
was to him unspeakably painful — as if it were a
treachery to the British flag. It was as unspeakably painful to him when later Casement, loath-
ing the Belgians so much for their treatment of
the natives on the Congo, took up arms against his
own country and was, to our eternal discredit,
hanged, rather than shot in the attempt to escape.
. . . We might have achieved *that* effort of our
wooden imaginations. . . .

It will be as well to attempt here some sort of
chronology. This is a novel exactly on the lines
of the formula that Conrad and the writer evolved.
For it became very early evident to us that what
was the matter with the Novel, and the British
novel in particular, was that it went straight forward, whereas in your gradual making acquaintanceship with your fellows you never do go
straight forward. You meet an English gentleman at your golf club. He is beefy, full of health,
the moral of the boy from an English Public
School of the finest type. You discover, gradually,
that he is hopelessly neurasthenic, dishonest in
matters of small change, but unexpectedly self-
sacrificing, a dreadful liar, but a most painfully

careful student of lepidoptera and, finally, from the public prints, a bigamist who was once, under another name, hammered on the Stock Exchange. . . . Still, there he is, the beefy, full-fed fellow, moral of an English Public School product. To get such a man in fiction you could not begin at his beginning and work his life chronologically to the end. You must first get him in with a strong impression, and then work backwards and forwards over his past. . . . That theory at least we gradually evolved.

At the beginning, then, of this chapter we had arrived at the year 1900 or so. We went to Knocke in Belgium and took up "Romance" once more, probably a year or so later; but Conrad's letter as to an endangered career was not written until about 1908. It comes in here as a light upon what did, upon what can have induced Conrad to desire to take a hand in the production of the book called "The Inheritors." . . .

Since the beginning of this chapter the writer has read a sufficiency of that work to satisfy him as to what it was all about. The process was distasteful, but the subordinating of one's nerves to duty is the first step towards a career or even towards the writing of a novel. And what made

Conrad passionately desirous of laying hands on
the writer's then subject was a sentence. One
sentence coming after an effective couple or so of
sentences with which the manuscript had opened.

—*—

The scene of that barratry is perfectly vivid to
the writer at this moment. He had driven over
to the Pent rather shyly with the manuscript of
the opening chapters of the novel in his pocket.
Conrad was as yet unaware that a novel was in
progress. He was sitting in the parlour of the
Pent with the monthly roses peeping just above the
window sill. After he had seen to the unharnessing of the disgraceful Exmoor pony — who had
only one accomplishment, that of undoing the bolt
of his oat chest with his teeth, which was a damna-
ble inconvenience, for the animal would fill itself
full to the lips with oats and then have to be walked
for seven or eight hours to save its life, and usually
in the dead of the night — after, then, the writer
had seen to the unharnessing of that plague, with
the aid of a disreputable, aged ex-time-serving
soldier called Hunt, who had had sunstroke, ague
and malaria in Quetta with the Buffs, who claimed
to be heir, in Chancery, of half the County of Kent,
who had always sore feet, hobbled, and whose
proximity resembled that of a rum-keg, and who
acted as our outdoor factotum and gardener, the

writer went into the parlour. Conrad was sitting reflecting and, beyond his saying, "My dear faller . . ." we did not speak. We were so constantly about each other's houses that quite often we could meet after driving over without any particular greeting, as if one of us had just come down from washing his hands in the bedroom. . . .

—*—

Conrad, then, was sitting gloomily reflecting— upon his career, upon the almost impossibility of wrestling any longer with the English that shall describe lagoons, shallows, brigs reflected in breathless water, upon the possibility that he would have to get over neck into debt before he should have finished "The Rescue"— a slight book almost no longer than a novelette, which was already mortgaged to Heinemann, that decent fellow who never worried his authors to complete their manuscripts. And there was the beginnings of another attack of gout in the right wrist; and Nancy needed shoeing. . . .

—*—

The writer then came in, and before sitting down drew the manuscript of the first chapter of "The Inheritors" from his pocket. Conrad said, "Another story . . . *Donne! Donne!*" Conrad had no particular admiration for the writer's

short stories. He had simply taken " Amy Foster "
from the writer, with no particular apology, and
had just rewritten it—introducing Amy herself,
who had not existed in the writer's draft. This,
however, was a novel, not a short story, and instead of giving the manuscript to Conrad, who
would merely have glanced at it perfunctorily and,
dropping it, would have returned to the contemplation of his debts and gout, the writer sat down
and began to read aloud.

———

At the end of the first paragraph Conrad said,
"*Mais mon cher, c'est très chic!* What is it? "
At the end of a sentence on the sixth page he was
exclaiming, " But what is this? What the devil
is this? It is *très, très, très chic!* It is *épatant.*
That's magnificent." And already the writer
knew that either he was in for another collaboration or that he would hand over the manuscript
altogether.

———

The sentence was:

I recovered my equanimity with the thought
that I had been visited by some stroke of an obscure and unimportant physical kind.

The opening paragraphs had run:

"Ideas," she said. "Oh, as for ideas—"
"Well," I hazarded, "as for ideas—"

We went through the old gateway and I cast a glance over my shoulder. The noon sun was shining over the masonry, over the little saints' effigies, over the little fretted canopies, the grime and the white streaks of bird-dropping. . . .

—*—

And as soon as the writer had let Conrad know that this was a novel, not a short story, he knew that he was in for another collaboration. Every word spoken added to that conviction. . . . The novel was to be a political work, rather allegorically backing Mr. Balfour in the then Government; the villain was to be Joseph Chamberlain who had made the war. The sub-villain was to be Leopold II, King of the Belgians, the foul — and incidentally lecherous — beast who had created the Congo Free State in order to grease the wheels of his harems with the blood of murdered negroes and to decorate them with fretted ivory cut from stolen tusks in the deep forests. . . . For the writer, until that moment, it had appeared to be an allegorico-realist romance; it showed the superseding of previous generations and codes by the merciless young who are always alien and without remorse. . . . But the moment Conrad spoke, he spoke with the voice of the Conrad who was avid of political subjects to treat and the writer knew that this indeed was the Conrad subject. . . .

II

"The Inheritors" is a work of seventy-five thousand words, as nearly as possible. In the whole of it there cannot be more than a thousand — certainly there cannot be two — of Conrad's writing; these crepitate from the emasculated prose like firecrackers amongst ladies' skirts.

I had looked at her before; now I cast a sideways, critical glance at her. I came out of my moodiness to wonder what type this was. *She had good hair, good eyes, and some charm. Yes.* And something besides — a something — a something *that was not an attribute of her beauty.* The modelling of her face was so perfect as to produce an effect of transparency, *yet there was no suggestion of frailness; her glance had an extraordinary strength of life. Her hair was fair and gleaming, her cheeks coloured* as if a warm light had fallen on them from somewhere. She was familiar till it occurred to you that she was strange.

━━

Do you not hear Conrad saying, "*Damn* Ford's women," and putting in, "She had good hair, good eyes and some charm." And do you not see **the** writer, at twenty-six, hitching and fitching with

"a something—a something—a something—"
to get an effect of delicacy, and Conrad saying,
"Oh, hang it all, do let's get some definite par-
ticulars about the young woman?"

—*—

That was how, normally, we collaborated. But
in this volume that is the only discoverable passage with which Conrad notably interfered. Occasionally he wrote in a whole speech that made
a situation. The difference between our methods
in those days was this: We both desired to get
into situations, at any rate when any one was
speaking, the sort of indefiniteness that is characteristic of all human conversations, and particularly of all English conversations that are
almost always conducted entirely by means of
allusions and unfinished sentences. If you listen
to two Englishmen communicating by means of
words, for you can hardly call it conversing, you
will find that their speeches are little more than
this: A. says, "What sort of a fellow is . . . *you*
know!" B. replies, "Oh, he's a sort of a . . ."
and A. exclaims, "Ah, I always thought so. . . ."
This is caused partly by sheer lack of vocabulary,
partly by dislike for uttering any definite statement at all. For anything that you say you may
be called to account. The writer really had a connection who said to one of her nieces, "My dear,

never keep a diary. It may one day be used against you," and that thought has a profound influence on English life and speech.

⟶

The writer used to try to get that effect by almost directly rendering speeches that, practically, never ended, so that the original draft of "The Inheritors" consisted of a series of vague scenes in which nothing definite was ever said. These scenes melted one into the other until the whole book, in the end, came to be nothing but a series of the very vaguest hints. The writer hoped by this means to get an effect of a sort of silverpoint: a delicacy. No doubt he succeeded. But the strain of reading him must have been intolerable.

⟶

Conrad's function in "The Inheritors" as it to-day stands was to give to each scene a final tap; these, in a great many cases, brought the whole meaning of the scene to the reader's mind. Looking through the book the writer comes upon instance after instance of these completions of scenes by a speech of Conrad's. Here you have the — quite unbearably vague — hero talking to the royal financier about the supernatural-adventuress heroine. Originally the speeches ran:

"You don't understand. . . . She. . . . She will. . . ."

He said: "Ah! Ah!" in an intolerable tone of royal badinage.

I said again: "You don't understand. . . . Even for your own sake. . . ."

He swayed a little on his feet and said: "Bravo. . . . Bravissimo. . . . You propose to frighten. . . ."

I looked at his great bulk of a body. . . . People began to pass, muffled up, on their way out of the place.

✦

The scene died away in that tone. In the book as it stands it runs, with Conrad's addition italicised:

"*If you do not*" (cease persecuting her had been implied several speeches before), *I said, "I shall forbid you to see her. And I shall. . . .*"

"*Oh, oh!*" *he interjected* with the intonation of a reveller at a farce. "We are at that—we are the excellent brother—" *He paused and then added: "Well, go to the devil, you and your forbidding." He spoke with the greatest good humour.*

"I am in earnest," I said, "very much in earnest. *The thing has gone too far.* And even for your own sake you had better. . . ."

He said: "Ah, ah!" in the tone of his "Oh, oh!"

"*She is no friend to you,*" I struggled on, "*she is playing with you for her own purposes;* you will. . . ."

He swayed a little on his feet and said: "*Bravo . . . bravissimo. If we can't forbid him we will frighten him. Go on, my good fellow. . . .*" and then, "*Come, go on.*"

I looked at his great bulk of a body. . . .

"*You absolutely refuse to pay any attention?*" I said.

"*Oh, absolutely,*" he answered.

At that point Conrad cut out a page or two of writing which was transferred to later in the book and came straight on to:

"Baron Halderschrodt has *committed suicide,*" which the writer for greater delicacy had rendered, "Baron Halderschrodt has . . ." Conrad, however, added still further to the effect by adding:

Half sentences came to our ears from groups that passed us: *A very old man with a nose that almost touched his thick lips was saying:*

"*Shot himself. . . . Through the left temple. . . . Mon Dieu!*"

If the reader asks how the writer identifies which was his writing and which Conrad's in a book nearly twenty-five years old, the answer is very simple. Partly the writer remembers. This was the only scene in the book at which we really hammered away for any time and the way we

did it is fresh still in his mind. Partly it is knowledge; Conrad would never have written "a very
old man" or "almost." He would have supplied
an image for the old man's nose and would have
given him an exact age, just as he had to precise
the fact that Halderschrodt had shot himself, and
through the left temple at that.

—✳—

The only other passage in the book that the
writer can quite definitely identify as Conrad's
is what follows. For the sake of the adventuress-
heroine and an income the lugubrious hero —
and this is the point — has betrayed to Mr. Chamberlain and the powers of evil, Mr. Balfour, Lord
Northcliffe, Leopold of Belgium, sound finance,
the small investor and the past. He is alone at
four in the morning with the drunken journalist,
the actual writer of the leader that produces these
sweeping results. The whole passage, which is
solid Conrad, is a matter of two pages. Here is
the most characteristic portion.

"You can't frighten me," I said. . . . "No
one can frighten me now." A sense of my in-
accessibility was the first taste of an achieved
triumph. I had done with fear. The poor devil
before me appeared infinitely remote. He was
lost; but he was only one of the lost: one of those
that I could see already overwhelmed by the rush

from the floodgates opened at my touch. He would be destroyed in good company; swept out of my sight together with the past they had known and with the future they had waited for. But he was odious. "I am done with you," I said.

"Eh, what? . . . Who wants to frighten? . . . I wanted to know what's your pet vice. . . . Won't tell? You might safely—I'm off. . . . Want me to tell mine? . . . No time. . . . I'm off. . . . Ask the policeman . . . crossing sweeper will do . . . I'm going."

"You will have to," I said.

"What. . . . Dismiss me? . . . Throw the indispensable Soane overboard like a squeezed lemon? . . . What would Fox say? . . . Eh? But you can't, my boy. Not you. Tell you . . . can't. . . . Beforehand with you . . . sick of it. . . . I'm off . . . to the Islands . . . the Islands of the Blest. . . . Come too . . . dismiss yourself out of all this. Warm sand, warm, mind you. You won't?" He had an injured expression. "Well, I'm off. See me into the cab, old chap, you're a decent fellow after all . . . not one of these beggars who would sell their best friend . . . for a little money . . . or some woman. Well, see me off."

. . . I went downstairs and watched him march up the street with a slight stagger under the pallid dawn. . . . The echo of my footsteps on the flagstones accompanied me, filling the empty earth with the sound of my footsteps.

That occurs nearly at the end of the book. There is one other passage of complete Conrad two pages further on:

I turned towards the river and on the broad embankment the sunshine enveloped me, friendly, familiar, warm like the care of an old friend. A black dumb-barge drifted, clumsy and empty, and the solitary man in it wrestled with the heavy sweep, straining his arms, throwing his face up to the sky at every effort. . . .
The barge with the man still straining at the oar has gone out of sight under the arch of the bridge, as through a gate into another world. A bizarre sense of solitude stole upon me and I turned my back upon the river as empty as my day. Hansoms, broughams, streamed with a continuous muffled roll of wheels and a beat of hoofs. A big dray put in a note of thunder and a clank of chains. . . .

Those two passages are practically all the Conrad writing that there is in the book. We must have had a severe struggle over those six or seven pages. That the writer realises because he remembers still the sense of relief that attended his writing the tremendously sentimental last scene, his wallowing in his own juvenile prose and his own dreadful sentences. As thus:

I had had my eyes on the ground all this while; now I looked at her, trying to realise that I should

never see her again. It was impossible. There
was that intense beauty, that shadowlessness that
was like translucence. And there was her voice.
It was impossible to understand that I was never
to see her again, never to hear her voice after
this.

She was silent for a long time and I said nothing
—nothing at all. . . . At last she said: "There
is no hope. We have to go our ways; you yours,
I mine. And then if you will—if you cannot
forget—you may remember that I cared; that,
for a moment, in between two breaths, I thought
of . . . of failing. That is all I can do . . . for
your sake." . . . I had not looked at her; but
stood with my eyes averted, very conscious of her
standing before me; of her great beauty, her great
glory.

The punctuation of this passage is that of the
uniform edition of the "Collected Works of Joseph
Conrad", the cover of which gives the book to
Joseph Conrad alone. The punctuation and the
misprints, which are very many, are American and
not the writer's. The rest is.

--*--

Having achieved this ending the writer carried
it over to the Pent. Conrad glanced at two or
three pages of the manuscript, exclaimed, "Marvellous! My dear boy. . . . My dear Ford.
Mon vieux, I don't know how you do it!" and

put the manuscript down on the table. The whole
went that afternoon to the printers.

—✳—

It has sometimes occurred to the writer to wonder whether Conrad ever read — ever could have
read — that passage. If he never did the omission
would have been all right. There was for excuse
the extreme fatigue of our struggle of wills that
went on whenever we really got down to a difficult passage; there was also the fact that the writer
was supposed to handle all the women in the books
we wrote together. . . . Conrad, however, assured
the writer that he had very carefully corrected the
proofs of the English Collected Edition of the
book, at a time when the writer was elsewhere employed. This was when he also asserted that "The
Inheritors" was a *damn* good book. And if we
add that he did let his name as sole author remain
on the cover of the book we must imagine that he
regarded it with *some* satisfaction. That his name
so appeared was of course no doing of Conrad's
but was due to the business talents of the late Mr.
Pinker and the publishers. (An author as a rule
is not shown the cover of his book before publication. And this is naturally more especially the
case when it is a matter of all the volumes of a
collected edition.) But Conrad offered to have
all the copies of "The Inheritors" and "Romance"

called in and the covers altered.   The writer,
however, said that it did not matter; as far as he
was concerned Conrad might have signed all his
books.   He might still.   So the edition was left
alone.   But at least Conrad did not mind the
attribution.

—⋇—

Nevertheless the writer prefers to believe that
Conrad never read the last chapter of "The Inheritors."   The factor of fatigue would be quite
enough to excuse it.   The writer is ready to confess that there are a few passages of "Romance"
that he himself has only read in French. . . . And
it was permitted to Conrad not to read the passages concerning what he called "Ford's women."
It had been only with something like nausea that
he had brought himself to approach this lady for
long enough to introduce the "she had good hair,
good eyes and some charm" of the opening quota-
tion of this chapter.   It was only with difficulty
that he was restrained from adding good teeth to
the catalogue.   He said with perfect seriousness,
"Why not good teeth?   Good teeth in a woman
are part of her charm.   Think of when she laughs.
You would not have her *not* have good teeth.   They
are a sign of health.   Your damn woman has to
be healthy, doesn't she?"   The writer, however,
stopped that. . . . To-day he would not.

Still the writer would rather believe that Conrad lied about the reading, about the proof-correcting, about anything; he would rather Conrad had robbed an alms box than that he should have read that dreadful prose and have called it damn good. The rest of the book is badly written but not so dreadfully. Still it is bad enough: a medley of prose conceived in the spirit of Christina Rossetti with imitations of the late Henry James; inspired by the sentimentality of a pre-Raphaelite actor is love scenes — precisely by Sir Johnston Forbes Robertson dyspeptically playing Romeo to Mrs. Patrick Campbell's Juliet; cadenced like Flaubert and full of little half-lines dragged in from the writer's own verses of that day. He was only twenty-six at the time and was very late in maturing. . . .

It runs like this: country atmosphere, romantic place-names and all:

We were sauntering along the forgotten valley that lies between Hardres and Stelling Minnis; we had been silent for several minutes. For me at least the silence was pregnant with . . . undefinable emotions. . . . There was something of the past world about the hanging woods, the little veils of unmoving mist — as if Time did not exist in those furrows of the great world; and one was so absolutely alone; (Conrad suddenly put in here:

anything might have happened. But the writer went on bravely.) I was silent. The birds were singing the sun down. It was very dark among the branches and from minute to minute the colours of the world deepened and grew sombre. . . . I was silent. A June nightingale began to sing, a trifle hoarsely. . . .

—⁂—

You perceive: the writer got his nightingale in after all: a marvel of oaken persistency. It may have been out of sheer agony that Conrad burst in here:

I stretched out my hand and it touched hers. I seized it without an instant of hesitation. "How could I resist you?" I said, and heard my own whisper with a sort of amazement at its emotion. . . .

Do not be alarmed. Anything *might* have happened. But the writer was there to save the young woman. Positively he remarks:

I did not know what it might lead to: I remembered that I did not know even who she was. . . . I let her hand fall. "We must be getting on," I said a trifle hoarsely. . . .

—⁂—

What then attracted Conrad to this farrago of nonsense? Partly no doubt it was the idea of getting a book finished quickly; here was another unexplored creek with possible gold in its shallows

or its huts. But it was only very partially that.
There was some mysterious attraction; Conrad's
manner was too animated, his enthusiasm too great
at the first reading. It may have been partly because the manuscript *was* read. The rhetorical
will pass when it comes in a human voice. The
writer has very frequently found good manuscripts that young men read to him, only to be
appalled by their ornamentation — or their bald-
ness, even! — when he afterwards read them for
himself. . . . Yet it cannot have been wholly that;
Conrad had opportunities enough of going through
the manuscript before the book was finished. Or
it may have been affection; Conrad may really
have had an affection for the writer. Yet it can
hardly have been that. . . .

The writer has sometimes imagined that, however much we might have scoffed at jewels five
words long that, on the stretched forefinger of old
time, sparkle for ever . . . however much we
might have scoffed, it was half-sentences of the
writer's that, inscrutably, jumped out of the prose
and caught Conrad by the throat. At the head of
this chapter stands the mysterious phrase, "Excellency, a few goats. . . ." The writer imagined
this. He wrote it in a quite commonplace frame
of mind, much as you might write an order for a

hoe when sending a list of agricultural instruments that you required to your ironmonger. He wanted to provide an obscure Lugareno with a plausible occupation. But no sooner had he got the words on the paper than Conrad burst into one of his roars of ecstasy. "This," he shouted when he was in a condition to speak, "is genius!" And out of breath, exhausted and rolling on the sofa, he continued to gasp, "Genius! . . . This is genius. . . . That's what it is. Pure genius. . . . Genius, I tell you!" The writer agreed that it *was* genius —for the sake of peace! And for twenty years afterwards, in every second or third letter to the writer Conrad returned to the charge. "Excellency, a few goats. . . ." he would write. "Do you remember?" Even this year in a letter to the *Transatlantic Review*, allotting parts of "Romance" to its various authors, he wrote, "Fifth Part, practically all yours, including the famous sentence at which we both exclaimed: This is genius! (Do you remember what it is?) with perhaps half a dozen lines by me. . . ."

In a subsequent number of the periodical in question the writer offered its readers as a prize a copy of "Romance" if any one of them could identify that passage of genius. A great many replies were received from readers offering passages of what, on the surface, looks more like genius. . . . But no one offered, "Excellency, a few goats. . . ." It is perhaps genius. But, frequently on receiving a "Don't you remember the few goats?" letter from Conrad the writer has felt as if he were getting credit for another immensely long shot at a rat. . . .

In "The Inheritors", then, there were several sentences which Conrad applauded almost as rapturously. There was the one already quoted about the stroke of an obscure and unimportant physical kind. . . . In that Conrad would like the words "obscure and unimportant." Another — it came after the passage concerning the suicide already quoted — is altogether the writer's and was in the first draft:

De Mersch walked slowly along the long corridor away from us. There was an extraordinary stiffness in his gait, as if he were trying to emulate the goose step of his old days in the Prussian Guard. My companion looked after him as though she wished to gauge the extent of his despair.

"You would say '*Habet*', wouldn't you?" she asked me.

This last sentence Conrad also called genius. Perhaps it may be.

"The Inheritors" appeared. It caused no excitement; even to ourselves it caused so little that the writer cannot so much as remember opening the parcel that contained the first copies. By that time Conrad had got over believing in its salable qualities; the writer had never had any delusions. He had been too well drilled by Mr. Edward Garnett.

It was received by the English critics with a pæan of abuse for the number of dots it contained. . . . One ingenious gentleman even suggested that we had cheated Mr. Heinemann and the public who had paid for a full six-shilling novel with words all solid on the page. In America it attracted even less attention, but the publishers, having issued the book with, as far as the writer can remember, a fault on the title page, or possibly on the cover, it was withdrawn after only four copies had been sold, and then reissued. These four copies are said to command an exorbitant price from collectors. The writer never remembers to have seen one.

III

We returned then to "Romance." . . .

It has been asserted that the writer paid Conrad large sums for the honour of collaborating with him, this being Conrad's inducement for continuing those very arduous labours. This was not the case. Even to lend money to Conrad was always a very difficult operation. Frequently it was a very painful one, seeing the agony of mind Conrad would be in over his debts or his complication of affairs; so that to be refused the ease to oneself of making a small loan had almost the aspect of a cruelty—as if a patient in great pain should refuse, for the sake of conscience, the alleviation of an anæsthetic. From the writer Conrad, except in one extreme case, never accepted any loan that he did not see his way plain to returning shortly and with an exact punctuality—and he always repaid on the date thus appointed by himself. The exception was a case of one of those complicated disasters that from time to time overwhelm those who have no means of making a livelihood, other than the frail, thin point of the pen. Conrad had been ill, there had been illness in his household. On top of it there came a bank smash, and Conrad was faced either with paying immediately a fairly substantial sum, or with being sold up. This sum the writer advanced to Conrad; it was in due time repaid.

＊

Illness and the anticipation of illness, debt, and still more the vision of the approach of a time when he must inevitably incur debt are, because of his necessary powers of the imagination, more terrible to the novelist than to any other human creature. As regards illness: In a society that has gradually become self-protectively organised the vocations or professions are very few in which the illness of a worker means entire cessation of income. The shopkeeper's shop will go on — perhaps it will be less efficiently conducted if its head is absent for any long period; and so with the business of the merchant or the financier. The doctor, the parson and the lawyer can find *locos tenentes* of course at some expense. The working man has his insurance; the serving class are to some extent protected by law. The literary man has nothing. Even insurance against illness is for him a very poor expedient since the things that will stop him working are as frequently as not diseases in no way diagnosable. The writer once suffered from a nervous breakdown that lasted for two years and over, during which he was withdrawn from practically all human activities, except taking the waters at various German Spas. He was completely unable to write. He had been insured against illness with a large and reputable society for a considerable time; yet all that he was able to recover, by way of a compromise, from that society was a sum a little less than a quarter of the instalments he had paid. There was no redress: apparently the laws of England hold that diseases of the nerves are not illnesses.

—*—

Yet they will stop you writing. And to so admirable a family man as was Conrad, half of whose mind at least was given to the matter of securing comfort and permanent provision for those dependent on him, whose agonies over this department of his life were sempiternal and overwhelming, the mere illness of a member of his family was sufficient to maim his working mind for long periods. For the author's mind jumps very fast to extreme apprehensions, and only too frequently he knows a great deal too much, for his peace of mind, of the progress of illnesses. He is forced to that by the very necessities of his profession in the course of which he must, from time to time at least, describe the progress of one illness or

another.   Indeed, he writes because his memory
is more tenacious and more vivid in its function-
ings than that of other men.   That causes the
anticipation of all misfortunes to weigh more
heavily on him.

—⋆—

That is if possible even more the case with the
facing of debts or the anticipation of debts.   The
layman incurs debts as a part of the necessary
business of life without which commercial opera-
tions cannot be conducted.   As often as not his
creditors are great corporations, unfeeling it is
true, but immune from personal suffering.   If he
himself goes bankrupt it is nowadays usually in
the form of a firm or a public company, and he
will go on much as before.   To the novelist a debt
is a sword in the hands of an individual who himself may starve if he do not receive his due, who
is also an executioner, who is also a mysterious
and dreaded force of evil, unknown in his function-
ings.   Unknown, particularly. . . . *What* happens
if you are county-courted?   What sort of faces
have broker's men?   Do they despise or reprove
you for having dared to incur a debt that you cannot discharge? . . . The pictured horrors of the
situation are infinite: you imagine your infant
child turned out of its cot by rough men like the
murderers in the Tower, or still more terribly,

you imagine your child old enough to appreciate deprivations, squalors, and the disgrace. . . .

—*—

Almost the most vivid emotion that the writer can remember in his whole life was caused by the first visit one of the greatest of writers paid to the Pent. It has been already described in a book of the writer's; but as no one discoverable ever read it it may come in here again. We were sitting then on a quiet sunlit day in the parlour of the Pent. Conrad was at the round table in the middle of the room, writing, his face to the window; his collaborator was reading some pages of corrected manuscript, facing into the room. A shadow went over those pages from the window behind. Conrad exclaimed, "Good God!" in an accent of such agony and terror that the writer's heart actually stopped as he swung round to the window to follow the direction of his companion's appalled glance. It went through his mind, "This must be the bailiff. . . . He has debts of which I do not know. . . . What's to be done? . . . Are all the doors bolted? . . . What does one do?"

An extremely tall man with a disproportionately small, grave head was stalking past the window, examining the house front with suspicion. . . . The family were all out driving. How could

they be got in if all the doors had to be bolted?
Through the window? But if a window is used
as a place of ingress surely a bailiff can use it too.
. . . One imagines that immense, grave fellow,
in a pepper-and-salt gamekeeper's coat with tails,
putting one knee over the window sill as a small
boy is handed in. . . . Surely an execution for
debt cannot take place after sunset? . . . Then
they will have to remain out till then. Or perhaps that is obsolete law. . . . They could go into
the great barn. . . . It is always warm and still
there, with the scent of hay: like an immense
church.

The house was perfectly still. The tall figure
with the aspect of a Spanish alcalde disappeared
from above the monthly roses. He had been
stalking, very slowly, like a man in a grave
pageant—a stork. Suddenly Conrad exclaimed
in a voice that was like a shout of joy, " By Jove!
. . . It's the man come about the mare!" Conrad
was almost always going through some complicated horse dealings with that mare of his. He was
going to exchange her for a pair of Shetland ponies
and a chaff-cutting machine; he was going to sell
her in Ashford market as against part of the price
of a stout Irish cob, the remainder to be paid by
the loaning of her during hay-making to the farmer

who hired the lands of the Pent; she was to be exchanged with a horse dealer who was shortly going out of business and had a most admirable roll-top desk and a really good typewriter. Traps could be hired from the Drum Inn at Stamford. . . .

Conrad's conviction restored life to the fainting Pent; it breathed once more; the cat jumped off the window sill; the clock struck four. . . . The writer hurried, a little tremulous still, to open the front door. . . . The tall, thin, grave man looked gravely at him. The writer exclaimed hurriedly, "The mare's out driving. . . ." He added, "With the ladies!" It's a great thing to be able to prove to a horse dealer that your mare can really be driven by a lady. The man—he resembled a sundial—said in the slow voice a sundial must have, "I'm Hudson!" The writer said, "Yes, yes. The mare's out with the ladies." Getting into his voice the resonance of a great bell, the tall man with the Spanish sort of beard said, "I'm . . . W. . . . H. . . . Hud . . . son. I want to see Conrad. You are not Conrad, are you? You are Hueffer." . . .

The writer may very well have psychologised Conrad wrongly, though he remains strongly un-

der the impression that after that king of men
had gone Conrad said, "By Jove, I thought he
was a bailiff!" But the occupation of writing to
such a nature as Conrad's is terribly engrossing.
To be suddenly disturbed is apt to cause a second's
real madness. . . . We were once going up to
Town in order to take some proofs to a publisher,
and halfway between Sandling and Charing Cross
Conrad remembered some phrase that he had forgotten to attend to in the proofs. He tried to
correct them with a pencil, but the train jolted so
badly that writing, sitting on a seat, was impossible.
Conrad got down on the floor of the carriage and
lying on his stomach went on writing. Naturally
when the one phrase was corrected twenty other
necessities for correction stuck out of the page.
We were alone in the carriage. The train passed
Paddock Wood, passed Orpington, rushed through
the suburbs. The writer said, "We're getting into
Town!" Conrad never moved except to write.
The house roofs of London whirled in perspective
round us; the shadow of Cannon Street Station
was over us. Conrad wrote. The final shadow
of Charing Cross was over us. It must have been
very difficult to see down there. He never moved.
. . . Mildly shocked at the idea that a porter
might open the carriage door and think us peculiar, the writer touched Conrad on the shoulder

and said, "We're there!" Conrad's face was most extraordinary—suffused and madly vicious. He sprang to his feet and straight at the writer's throat. . . .

—✴—

The lay reader—say an officer of His Majesty's Army—should not here say, "Ah, these literary men!" . . . Let him think of his own feelings when he is trying to write some particularly complicated lie in an excuse to Orderly Room over something or other. . . . The writer once saw a colonel—and a deuced smart colonel at that—in Orderly Room, snatch up a revolver and *damn* near shoot an orderly who had interrupted him in a literary composition. The Quartermaster whose job it was, the Adjutant, and the writer, who had been called in, having all failed, the C.O. was himself trying to explain to garrison headquarters why the regiment's washing was given to the Riverdale Laundry Company instead of to some firm recommended by G. H. Z. You could almost swear his tongue followed his pen round and round in his mouth in the effort of composition. . . .

—✴—

Well, the lay reader should understand that *our* tongues really do follow our pens when we are engaged in writing the specious lies on which our existence depends. And if our lies are not con-

vincing, we, even as he, shall starve. And we are
at it all the time whilst he gives on an average not
more than five minutes a day for five days of the
week to composing the misleading documents that
save him from having to resign his commission.
And he has only one Orderly Room and only one
Assistant Adjutant to deceive: we lie to thousands.
If we are lucky, to tens of thousands! So we are
engrossed. . . . It is not more easy for us to put
words together; it is more difficult because we have
more sense of words. And we who go at it with
persistence, undespairing, in the face of inevitable
failure . . . are the gallant spirits.

Conrad at least was. It has to be remembered
that he had to wrestle, not with one language only,
but with three. Or, say with two and the ghost
of one, for it happened to him occasionally to say,
"There's a word *so and so* in Polish to express
what I want." But that happened only very seldom. All the rest of the time he got an effect to
satisfy himself in French. This was of course the
case preponderantly in passages of some nicety of
thought and expression. He could naturally write,
"Will you have a cup of tea?" or "He is dead,"
without first expressing himself to himself in
French. But when he wrote a set of phrases like
"the gift of expression", "the bewildering", "the

illuminating ", "the most exalted ", "the most con-
temptible ", "the pulsating stream of light", or
"the deceitful flow from the heart of an impene-
trable darkness ", he was translating directly from
the French in his mind. Or when he wrote, "Their
glance was guileless, profound, confident and trust-
ing ", or, "The offing was barred by a black bank
of clouds, and the tranquil waterway leading to the
uttermost ends of the earth flowed sombre under
an overcast sky — seemed to lead into the heart of
an immense darkness." Naturally, as a British
master mariner, he did not *have* to think of the
offing as "*le large*", but when he was trying the
sound of that sentence for his final cadence he
did first say "*le large*" and then said, "The open
sea; the *way* to the open sea. No, the *offing.*"
That the writer very well remembers. . . . Conrad moreover had for long intended to end the
story with the words, "The horror! The horror!"
"*L'horreur!*" having been the last words of Kurtz;
but he gave that up. The accentuation of the
English word was different from the French;
the shade of meaning, too. And the device of such
an ending, which would have been quite normal in
a French story, would have been what we used to
call *chargé* — a word meaning something between
harrowing, melodramatic, and rhetorical, for
which there is no English equivalent. Perhaps

"overloaded with sentiment" would come as near it as you can get: but that is clumsy. . . .

---*---

But the mere direct translation from imagined French into English was just child's play. It was when you came to the transposing precisely, of such a word as *chargé* from French into English, that difficulties began. The writer remembers Conrad spending nearly a whole day over one word in two or three sentences of proofs for the Blackwood volume called "Youth." It was two words, perhaps—serene and azure. Certainly it was azure. "And she crawled on, do or die, in the serene weather. The sky was a miracle of purity, a miracle of azure." Conrad said, a*zure*, the writer *ay*sure—or more exactly *ay*syeh. This worried Conrad a good deal since he wanted a*zure* for his cadence. He read the sentence over and over again to see how it sounded.

---*---

The point was that he was perfectly aware that azure was a French word, or in English almost exclusively a term of heraldry, and his whole endeavour was given to using only such words as are found in the normal English vernacular—or thereabouts, for he never could be got really to believe how poverty-stricken a thing the normal English vernacular is. The vocabulary that he used in speaking English was enormous and he regarded it as a want of patriotism to think that the average Englishman knew his language less well than himself.

—⋆—

Mr. Henry James used to call Marlowe, the usual narrator for many years of Conrad's stories, "that preposterous master mariner." He meant precisely that Marlowe was more of a philosopher and had a vocabulary vastly larger and more varied than you could possibly credit to the master mariner as a class. Conrad, however, persisted that Marlowe was little above the average of the ship's officer in either particular, and presumably he knew his former service mates better than did Mr. James—or the rest of us. . . . Still he *did* think that the word azure would be outside the ordinary conversational vocabulary of a ship's captain. . . .

—⋆—

We talked about it then for a whole day. . . . Why not say simply "blue"? Because really, it is not blue. Blue is something coarser in the grain; you imagine it the product of the French Impressionist painter—or of a house painter—with the brush strokes showing. Or you think so of blue after you have thought of azure. Azure is more transparent. . . .

Or again the word "serene." . . . Why not calm? Why not quiet? . . . Well, quiet as applied to weather is — or perhaps it is only was — part of the "little language" that was being used by the last Pre-Raphaelite poets. That ruled quiet out. Calm on the other hand is, to a master mariner, almost too normal and too technically inclusive. Calm is in a log-book almost any weather that would not be agitating to a landsman — or thereabouts. Dead calm is — again to a seaman — too technical. Dead calmness precludes even the faintest ruffle of wind, even the faintest cat's-paw on the unbroken surface of the sea.

⸺

The writer has heard it objected that Conrad was pernicketty; why should he not use technical sea terms and let the reader make what he could of it? But Conrad's sea is more real than the sea of any other sea writer; and it is more real, because he avoided the technical word.

⸺

The whole passage of "Youth" under consideration is as follows — the writer is quoting from memory, but as far as this passage is concerned he is fairly ready to back his memory against the printed page:

And she crawled on, do or die, in the serene weather. The sky was a miracle of purity, a miracle of azure. The sea was polished, was blue, was pellucid, was sparkling like a precious stone, extending on all sides, all round to the horizon. As if the whole terrestrial globe had been one jewel, one colossal sapphire. And on the lustre of the great calm waters the *Judea* moved imperceptibly, enveloped in languid and unclean vapours. . . .

That is as far as the writer's memory will carry him, though the paragraph ends with the words, " The splendour of sea and sky."

This then is almost the perfection of sea writing of its type. (Stephen Crane could achieve another perfection by writing of the waves as barbarous and abrupt: but that in the end is no less anthropomorphic.) And the words serene and azure remained after an infinite amount of talking so that the whole passage might retain its note of the personality of Destiny that watched inscrutably behind the sky. It was Destiny that was serene, that had purity, that was azure . . . and that ironically set that smudge of oily vapour from the burning vessel across the serenity of the miraculous sapphire — so that youth might be enlightened as to the nature of the cosmos, even whilst in process of being impressed with its splendours.

" Serene " as applied to weather; " azure " as

applied to the sky are over-writing a shade, are a shade *chargés* if they apply merely to the sea and merely to the sky. . . . But Conrad was obsessed by the idea of a Destiny omnipresent behind things; of a Destiny that was august, blind, inscrutable, just, and above all passionless, that has decreed that the outside things — the sea, the sky, the earth, love, merchandising, the winds — shall make youth seem tenderly ridiculous and all the other ages of men gloomy, imbecile, thwarted — and possibly heroic. . . . Had the central character of this story been a fortyish man you would have had, added to the burning ship with its fumes, dirty weather, dripping clothes, the squalid attributes of the bitter sea. As it was an affair of *youth* you have serene weather and a miracle of purity, to enhance the irony of Destiny.

Part III

IT IS ABOVE ALL TO MAKE
YOU SEE. . . .

I

THE time has come, then, for some sort of critical estimate of this author. Critical, not philosophical. For the philosophy of Joseph Conrad was a very simple one; you might sum it all up in the maxim of Herrick's: To live merrily and trust to good letters. Himself he summed it up in the great word "Fidelity", and his last great novel turned upon a breach of trust by his typical hero, his King Tom. It is the misfortune of morality that the greatest thrills that men can get from life come from the contemplation of its breaches!

·——·

About Conrad there was, however, as little of the moralist as there was of the philosopher. When he had said that every work of art has — must have — a profound moral purpose, and he said that every day and all day long, he had done with the subject. So that the writer has always wished that Conrad had never written his famous message on Fidelity. Truly, those who read him knew his conviction that the world, the temporal world, rests on a very few simple ideas — and it might have been left at that. For it was the very basis of all Conrad's work that the fable must not have the moral tacked on to its end. If the fable has not driven its message home the fable has failed, must be scrapped and must give place to another one.

—☀—

But the impulse to moralise, to pontify, is a very strong one, and comes in many treacherous guises. One may so easily do it unawares: and instances of Conrad's pontifications are far enough to seek, considering the temporal eminence to which he attained. He let, otherwise, his light so shine before men that few would be inclined to claim him amongst the preachers.

—☀—

He was before all things the artist and his chief message to mankind is set at the head of this chapter. . . . " It is above all things to make you *see*. . . ." Seeing is believing for all the doubters of this planet, from Thomas to the end: if you can make humanity see the few very simple things upon which this temporal world rests you will make mankind believe such eternal truths as are universal. . . .

—☀—

That message, that the province of written art is above all things to make you see, was given before we met; it was because that same belief was

previously and so profoundly held by the writer
that we could work for so long together. We had
the same aims and we had all the time the same
aims. Our attributes were no doubt different.
The writer probably knew more about words, but
Conrad had certainly an infinitely greater hold
over the architectonics of the novel, over the way
a story should be built up so that its interest progresses and grows up to the last word. Whether
in the case of our officially collaborated work or
in the work officially independent in which we
each modified the other with almost as much enthusiasm and devotion as we gave to work done
together, the only instance that comes to the
writer's mind in which he of his own volition
altered the structure of any work occurred in the
opening chapters of " The Rescue."

Of that book Conrad made many drafts, over
a very great number of years. The writer seems
to remember, but is not quite certain, having
heard Conrad say that he had meant to take up
the story of " The Rescue " immediately after the
publication or the finishing of " Almayer's Folly."
And it obviously belongs to the group of subjects
set in Malaysia or thereabouts, of the date, say, of
" Karain " from " Tales of Unrest ", or " The La-
goon ", that was published in the same volume,

dated 1898. (In the matter of books published in London in the nineties, dates of publication, if these are of any importance, are sometimes hazy. Thus the writer's first book was published in 1891, but the date given on the title page is 1892. The ingenious publisher, who was also Conrad's, hit on this stratagem, afterwards imitated by American magazines, with the idea of beguiling the possible buyer into the belief that he was purchasing a brand new book eighteen months or so after it had been published.) "Karain", then, the one of his early short stories that Conrad liked best, was published in *Blackwood's* in 1897 and then in a volume that is dated 1898. It was, as far as the writer's memory serves him, written in 1896.

—*—

The relationship of "Karain" to "The Rescue" is obvious. For two years Conrad carried the idea of the novel about with him and then, after the publication of "The Nigger of the Narcissus" by Heinemann in 1898, he definitely sketched the plot of "The Rescue" to Heinemann himself. On this sketch he obtained one of his advances from that kindly man. Immediately afterwards he began his first draft of the novel. . . .

—*—

That advance remained an old man of the mountain for years and years. There were the glorious schemes for finishing off such and such a book by such and such a date and then quickly writing two or three stories like "Gaspar Ruiz" for a periodical that paid great prices, thus getting free forever of indebtedness! . . . Then there came always the grim remembrance, "There's that advance of Heinemann's on 'The Rescue.' . . ." That no doubt rather hypnotised his will when he attacked, as he constantly did, that particular book. He made at least six separate beginnings of a chapter, or a chapter and a half each, with every different kind of arrangement of paragraphs and openings. At last, towards 1906, Conrad, in one of his crises of rearrangement had got his affairs nearly straightened out. He then once more remembered with despair Heinemann's advance which, together with "The Rescue" itself, had remained out of sight for four or five years. So the writer said to Conrad, "You'd better give me those manuscripts and let me put together some sort of a beginning for you." Conrad was then wrestling with the opening chapter of "Chance" which he expected with any luck to finish, slight affair as it was going to be, in about three months. It was actually finished seven years later.

—*—

Openings for us, as for most writers, were

matters of great importance, but probably we
more than most writers realised of what primary
importance they were. A real short story must
open with a breathless sentence; a long-short story
may begin with an " as " or a " since " and some leisurely phrases. At any rate the opening paragraph
of book or story should be of the tempo of the
whole performance. That is the *règle generale*.
Moreover, the reader's attention must be gripped
by that first paragraph. So our ideal novel must
begin either with a dramatic scene or with a note
that should suggest the whole book. " The Nigger
of the Narcissus " begins:

Mr. Baker, chief mate of the *Narcissus*, stepped
in one stride out of his lighted cabin into the darkness of the quarter deck. . . .

" The Secret Agent ":

Mr. Verloc, going out in the morning, left
his shop nominally in charge of his brother-in-
law. . . .

" The End of the Tether ":

For a long time after the course of the steamer
Sophala had been altered. . . .

this last being the most fitting beginning for the
long-short story that " The End of the Tether " is.

" Romance ", on the other hand begins:

To yesterday and to to-day I say my polite

vaya usted con dios. What are those days to me?
But that far-off day of my romance, when from
between the blue and white bales in Don Ramon's
darkened store room in Kingston. . . .

an opening for a long novel in which the dominant
interest lies far back in the story and the note must
be struck at once.

"The Inheritors" first lines are:

"Ideas," she said. "Oh, as for ideas . . ."

an opening for a short novel.

—*—

Conrad's tendency and desire made for the
dramatic opening; the writer's as a rule for the
more pensive approach; but we each, as a book
would go on, were apt to find that we must modify
our openings. This was more often the case with
Conrad than with the writer, since Conrad's books
depended much more on the working out of an
intrigue which he would develop as the book was
in writing: the writer has seldom begun on a book
without having, at least, the intrigue, the "affair",
completely settled in his mind.

—*—

The disadvantage of the dramatic opening is
that after the dramatic passage is done you have
to go back to getting your characters in, a proceeding that the reader is apt to dislike. The danger
with the reflective opening is that the reader is apt

to miss being gripped at once by the story. Openings are therefore of necessity always affairs of
compromise.

The note should here be struck that in all the
conspiracies that went on at the Pent or round
the shores of the Channel there was absolutely no
mystery. We thought just simply of the reader.
Would this passage grip him? If not it must go.
Will this word make him pause and so slow down
the story? If there is any danger of that, away
with it. That is all that is meant by the dangerous
word *technique*.

Tremendous readers, both of us, we tried to
gather from the books we had read what made
one book readable and the other not. English
gentlemen of the Palmerston days, there was no
nonsense about us; we tried to turn out the sort
of book that, from "Lady Audley's Secret" to
Boswell's "Johnson", and from "Midshipman
Easy" to "Education Sentimentale", the English
gentleman might read in his library, with the
cedar trees on the lawn outside it—or the flag
lieutenant, in harbour, during the dogwatches.

We had the intimate conviction that two and
only two classes of books are of universal appeal:

the very best and the very worst. The very worst, securing immediate attention by way of some trick, gradually fade from the public memories; the very best, being solid and shipshape productions of solid and shipshape men with no nonsense about them, remain. We attempted then to turn out solid and shipshape books.

There was really nothing more to it, Conrad being the more solid, the more shipshape and the more determined of the two, the writer being the more tenacious. . . . "You have a perfect right to say that you are rather unchangeable," Conrad wrote not long before his end, " Unlike the serpent (which is Wise) you will die in your original skin." . . . That is to say that the writer never made concessions. We elaborated certain principles and the writer saw to it that we did work along those lines. Conrad would occasionally try to rush a position, being worn out by the long drag of work. That is why the ends of his books have sometimes the air of being rather slight compared with the immense fabrics to which they are the appendages. In effect, Conrad was the more determined — to get something done; the writer, more listless, never cared much whether a thing were done or not. He insisted, however, that if it were done it should be done to contract.

It was a combination not really unfortunate. The cases must be rare in which one man of letters can have had at his disposal for a number of years the whole brain of another man of letters of an unpliant disposition. Conrad so had the writer's. For it was quite definitely the writer's conviction that the only occupation fitting for a proper man in these centuries is the writing of novels — and that no novel worth much could be written by himself or any other man — at any rate, by himself — before he has reached the age of forty. So till he had attained that age the writer was determined never to attempt the production of anything that was not either a pastiche or a *tour de force* — just for practice in writing. One must roll one's hump around the world first. . . . Thus, rather listlessly and a little disdainfully, from time to time the writer turned out historical novels — which were received with very great acclamations — and books of connected essays that were received with acclamations almost greater. But the writer was not disturbed; a historical novel even at the best is nothing more than a *tour de force*, a fake more or less genuine in inspiration and workmanship, but none the less a fake. Even " Salammbo " is that. A book of connected essays . . . well, it is not a novel! In addition the writer did attempt two pastiches in the manner of Mr. Henry

James, written, one of them, as a variation on a book of essays to give the effect of a tour in the United States — an international affair. The other was the product of an emotion, as you get over things by writing them down in your diary.

—✳—

From time to time gentlemen of the Press anxious to depreciate the writer have said that he imitated the work of Conrad. This was not the case. It is a curious characteristic of the work of Conrad that, not only can you not recognisably imitate it, you hardly ever feel even the impulse to do so, and the one writer who really sedulously be-aped the more exotic romances of the author of "An Outpost of Progress" achieved performances so lugubrious that he seems to have warned off any other imitators of his example. The fact is that Conrad, like Turgenev, is very little mannered; his temperament had no eccentricities that could be easily imitated; his vocabulary was as much the result of difficulties as of arbitrary selection; his cadences were so intimately his own that they were practically unimitable. The writer probably more than any other man must have had opportunities of studying the way prose came to Conrad but the writer does not remember more than three sentences that he ever wrote — apart from sentences that he actually composed for Con-

rad himself — in which he either consciously tried
for some purpose or other to get the cadence of a
sentence of Conrad's, or as to which he felt, after
having written them, the satisfaction which he
might imagine himself feeling if he *had* written
a Conrad sentence.   If the accusation had been of
imitation of Mr. Henry James it might have been
just enough, though a pastiche is not exactly the
same thing as an imitation, being an exercise in
the manner of a writer rather than an attempt to
make a living by concealed plagiarism. . . .

Still, whatever may have been the writer's oc-
cupations, he was ready to be pulled off them at
any moment at the instance of Conrad's necessities.
And this probably *was* of service to the author of
"The Rescue." . . . As regards the opening of
that book the writer very well remembers how the
rearrangement was made. . . . In all Conrad's
drafts the opening was dramatic.   In most of them
it began with a speech of Tom Lingard's, one of
them with the words, "You've been sleeping —
you.   Shift the helm.   She has got stern way on
her."   One version even began as far back, in the
book as it stands at present, as an interview between
Lingard and Mrs. Travers. . . . Conrad had
meant that to be the dramatic opening; in that case
he would have had to introduce an immense retro-

spection giving the biographies of Lingard, of
Carter, of the Travers, of Jaffir, of the Malay
serangs . . . of everybody and everything.

—*—

On the impracticability of that we both agreed
and the writer took the various drafts away to
Aldington to study. A good many of the drafts
that the writer made opened with a passage of
description, "Out of the level blue of a shallow
sea Carimata raises a lofty barrenness of grey and
yellow tints, the drab eminence of its arid heights,"
the writer thinking that a slow passage of geographical significance ought, logically, to open
what seemed likely to be a very long book. Then
one day it occurred to him to ask, "Why, after all,
not have a historical opening and so avoid, later
on, the necessity to slow the story down in order to
get in the history?" So at the opening, at any rate
of one draft, of chapter two, he found the passage
beginning, "The shallow sea that foams and mur-
murs on the shores of the thousand islands, big and
little, which make up the Malay Archipelago has
been for centuries the scene of adventurous under-
takings."

—*—

And all this passage seeming to him to be admirable, beautiful and engrossing prose, it struck
him that it might be relied on at once to grip

the reader's attention and to give the note of the coming story. So in "The Rescue" you have the opening historical passage, the geographical passage and then Lingard's words:

"You've been sleeping—you. Shift the helm. She has got stern way on her."

II

It might be as well here to put down under separate headings, such as "Construction", "Development", and the like, what were the formulæ for the writing of the novel at which Conrad and the writer had arrived, say in 1902 or so, before we finally took up and finished "Romance." The reader will say that that is to depart from the form of the novel in which form this book pretends to be written. But that is not the case. The novel more or less gradually, more or less deviously, lets you into the secrets of the characters of the men with whom it deals. Then, having got them in, it sets them finally to work. Some novels, and still more short stories, will get a character in with a stroke or two as does Maupassant in the celebrated sentence in the "Reine Hortense" which Conrad and the writer were never tired of — quite intentionally — misquoting: "*C'était un monsieur à favoris rouges qui entrait toujours le premier. . . .*" He was a gentleman with red whiskers who always went first through a doorway. . . . *That* gentleman is so sufficiently got in that you need know no more of him to understand how he will act. He has been "got in" and can get to work at once. That is called by the official British critics the static method and is, for some reason or other, contemned in England.

———⋆———

Other novels, however, will take much, much longer to develop their characters. Some—and this one is an example—will take almost a whole book to really get their characters in and will then dispose of the "action" with a chapter, a line, or even a word—or two. The most wonderful instance of all of that is the ending of the most wonderful of all Maupassant's stories, "Champs d'Oliviers", which, if the reader has not read, he should read at once. Let us now take a heading. (This method has the advantage that the lay reader who cannot interest himself in literary methods and the Critic-Annalist whose one passion is to cut the cackle and come to the horses can skip the whole chapter, certain that he will miss none of the spicy titbits.)

General Effect

We agreed that the general effect of a novel must be the general effect that life makes on mankind. A novel must therefore not be a narration, a report. Life does not say to you: In 1914 my next-door neighbour, Mr. Slack, erected a greenhouse and painted it with Cox's green aluminum paint. . . . If you think about the matter you will remember, in various unordered pictures, how one day Mr. Slack appeared in his garden and contemplated the wall of his house. You will then try to remember the year of that occurrence and you will fix it as August, 1914, because having had the foresight to bear the municipal stock of the City of Liège you were able to afford a first-class season ticket for the first time in your life. You will remember Mr. Slack — then much thinner because it was before he found out where to buy that cheap Burgundy of which he has since drunk an inordinate quantity, though whisky you think would be much better for him! Mr. Slack again came into his garden, this time with a pale, weaselly-faced fellow, who touched his cap from time to time. Mr. Slack will point to his house wall several times at different points, the weaselly fellow touching his cap at each pointing. Some days after, coming back from business, you will have observed against Mr. Slack's wall. . . . At this point you will remember that you were then the manager of the fresh-fish branch of Messrs. Catlin and Clovis in Fenchurch Street. . . . What a change since then! Millicent had not yet put her hair up. . . . You will remember how Millicent's hair looked, rather pale and burnished in

plaits.   You will remember how it now looks,
henna'd; and you will see in one corner of your
mind's eye a little picture of Mr. Mills the vicar
talking—oh, very kindly—to Millicent after she
has come back from Brighton. . . . But perhaps
you had better not risk that. You remember some
of the things said by means of which Millicent
has made you cringe—and her expression! . . .
Cox's Aluminum Paint! . . . You remember the
half-empty tin that Mr. Slack showed you—he
had a most undignified cold—with the name in a
horseshoe over a blue circle that contained a red
lion asleep in front of a real-gold sun. . . .

And, if that is how the building of your neighbour's greenhouse comes back to you, just imagine
how it will be with your love affairs that are so
much more complicated. . . .

IMPRESSIONISM

We accepted without much protest the stigma
"Impressionists" that was thrown at us. In those
days Impressionists were still considered to be bad
people: Atheists, Reds, wearing red ties with which
to frighten householders.   But we accepted the
name because Life appearing to us much as the
building of Mr. Slack's greenhouse comes back
to you, we saw that Life did not narrate, but made
impressions on our brains.   We in turn, if we

wished to produce on you an effect of life, must
not narrate but render impressions.

SELECTION

We agreed that the whole of Art consists in selection. To render your remembrance of your
career as a fish salesman might enhance the story
of Mr. Slack's greenhouse, or it might *not*. A
little image of iridescent, blue-striped, black-
striped, white fish on a white marble slab with
water trickling down to them round a huge mass
of orange salmon roe; a vivid description of a horrible smell caused by a cat having stolen and
hidden in the thick of your pelargoniums a cod's
head that you had brought back as a perquisite, you
having subsequently killed the cat with a hammer,
but long, long before you had rediscovered her
fishy booty. . . . Such little impressions might be
useful as contributing to illustrate your character
— one should not kill a cat with a hammer! They
might illustrate your sense of the beautiful — or
your fortitude under affliction — or the disagree-
ableness of Mr. Slack, who had a delicate sense of
smell — or the point of view of your only daughter,
Millicent.

We should then have to consider whether your
sense of the beautiful or your fortitude could in

our rendering carry the story forward or interest the reader. If it did we should include it; if in our opinion it was not likely to, we should leave it out. Or the story of the cat might in itself seem sufficiently amusing to be inserted as a purposed *longueur*, so as to give the idea of the passage of time. . . . It may be more amusing to read the story of a cat with your missing dinner than to read, "A fortnight elapsed. . . ." Or it might be better after all to write boldly, "Mr. Slack, after a fortnight had elapsed, remarked one day very querulously, 'That smell seems to get worse instead of better.'"

SELECTION (SPEECHES)

That last would be compromise, for it would be narration instead of rendering: it would be far *better* to give an idea of the passage of time by picturing a cat with a cod's head, but the length of the story must be considered. Sometimes to render anything at all in a given space will take up too much room — even to render the effect and delivery of a speech. Then just boldly and remorselessly you must relate and *risk* the introduction of yourself as author, with the danger that you may destroy all the illusion of the story.

Conrad and the writer would have agreed that

the ideal rendering of Mr. Slack's emotions would
be as follows:

A scrawny, dark-brown neck, with an immense
Adam's apple quivering over the blue stripes of
a collar, erected itself between the sunflower stems
above the thin oaken flats of the dividing fence.
An unbelievably long, thin gap of a mouth opened
itself beneath a black-spotted handkerchief, to say
that the unspeakable odour was sufficient to slay
all the porters in Covent Garden. Last week it
was only bad enough to drive a regiment of dragoons into a faint. The night before the people
whom he had had to supper — I wondered who
could eat any supper with any appetite under the
gaze of those yellow eyes — people, mind you, to
whom he had hoped to sell a little bit of property
in the neighbourhood. Good people. With more
than a little bit in the bank. People whose residence would give the whole neighbourhood a lift.
They had asked if he liked going out alone at night
with so many undiscovered murders about. . . .
"Undiscovered murders!" he went on repeating,
as if the words gave him an intimate sense of relief.
He concluded with the phrase, "I *don't* think!"

That would be a very fair *rendering* of part of
an episode: it would have the use of getting quite
a lot of Mr. Slack in; but you might want to get
on towards recounting how you had the lucky idea
of purchasing shares in a newspaper against which

Mr. Slack had counselled you. . . . And you might have got Mr. Slack in already!

—✦—

The rendering in fact of speeches gave Conrad and the writer more trouble than any other department of the novel whatever. It introduced at once the whole immense subject of under what convention the novel is to be written. For whether you tell it direct and as author — which is the more difficult way — or whether you put it into the mouth of a character — which is easier by far but much more cumbersome — the question of reporting or rendering speeches has to be faced. To pretend that any character or any author writing directly can remember whole speeches with all their words for a matter of twenty-four hours, let alone twenty-four years, is absurd. The most that the normal person carries away of a conversation after even a couple of hours is just a salient or characteristic phrase or two, and a mannerism of the speaker. Yet, if the reader stops to think at all, or has any acuteness whatever, to render Mr. Slack's speech directly, " Thet there odour is enough to do all the porters in Common Gorden in. Lorst week it wouldn' no more 'n 'v sent a ole squad of tinwiskets barmy on the crumpet . . ." and so on through an entire monologue of a page and a half, must set the reader at some point or other wondering how the author or the narrator can possibly, even if they were present, have remembered every word of Mr. Slack's long speech. Yet the object of the novelist is to keep the reader entirely oblivious of the fact that the author exists —even of the fact that he is reading a book. This is of course not possible to the bitter end, but a reader *can* be rendered very engrossed, and the nearer you can come to making him entirely insensitive to his surroundings, the more you will have succeeded.

—⋆—

Then again, directly reported speeches in a book do move very slowly; by the use of indirect locutions, together with the rendering of the effects of other portions of speech, you can get a great deal more into a given space. There is a type of reader that likes what is called conversations— but that type is rather the reader in an undeveloped state than the reader who has read much. So, wherever practicable, we used to arrange speeches much as in the paragraph devoted to Mr. Slack above. But quite often we compromised and gave passages of direct enough speech.

—⋆—

This was one of the matters as to which the writer was more uncompromising than was Conrad. In the novel which he did at last begin on

his forty-first birthday there will be found to be
hardly any direct speech at all, and probably none
that is more than a couple of lines in length. Conrad indeed later arrived at the conclusion that, a
novel being in the end a matter of convention —
and in the beginning too, for the matter of that,
since what are type, paper, bindings and all the
rest, but matters of agreement and convenience —
you might as well stretch convention a little farther,
and postulate that your author or your narrator is a
person of a prodigious memory for the spoken.
He had one minute passion with regard to conversations: he could not bear the repetition of " he
said's " and " she said's ", and would spend agitated
hours in chasing those locutions out of his or our
pages and substituting "he replied", "she ejacu-
lated", "answered Mr. Verloc" and the like.
The writer was less moved by this consideration;
it seemed to him that you could employ the words
"he said " as often as you like, accepting them as
being unnoticeable, like "a", "the", "his", "her",
or "very."

CONVERSATIONS

One unalterable rule that we had for the rendering of conversations — for genuine conversations
that are an exchange of thought, not interrogatories
or statements of fact — was that no speech of one

character should ever answer the speech that goes before it. This is almost invariably the case in real life where few people listen, because they are always preparing their own next speeches. When, of a Saturday evening, you are conversing over the fence with your friend Mr. Slack, you hardly notice that he tells you he has seen an incredibly coloured petunia at a market gardener's, because you are dying to tell him that you have determined to turn author to the extent of writing a letter on local politics to the newspaper of which, against his advice, you have become a large shareholder.

He says, "Right down extraordinary that petunia was . . . ."

You say, "What would you think now of my . . . ."

He says, "Diamond-shaped stripes it had, blue-black and salmon. . . . ."

You say, "I've always thought I had a bit of a gift. . . . ."

Your daughter Millicent interrupts, "Julia Gower has got a pair of snake-skin shoes. She bought them at Wiston and Willocks's."

—⋆—

You miss Mr. Slack's next two speeches in wondering where Millicent got that bangle on her wrist. You will have to tell her more carefully than ever that she must *not* accept presents from Tom, Dick and Harry. By the time you have come out of that reverie Mr. Slack is remarking:

"I said to him use turpentine and sweet oil, three parts to two. What do you think?"

SURPRISE

We agreed that the one quality that gave interest to Art was the quality of surprise. That is very well illustrated in the snatch of conversation just given. If you reported a long speech of Mr. Slack's to the effect that he was going to enter some of his petunias for the local flower show and those, with his hydrangeas and ornamental sugar-beet, might well give him the Howard Cup for the third time in which case it would become his property out and out. He would then buy two silver and cut-glass epergnes, one to stand on each side of the Cup on his sideboard. He always did think that a touch of silver and cut glass. . . . If, after that, you gave a long speech of your own — after, naturally, you had added a few commonplaces as a politeness to Mr. Slack—if you gave a long speech in which with modesty you dwelt on the powers of observation and of the pen that you had always considered yourself to possess, and in which you announced that you certainly meant to write a letter to the paper in which you had shares — on the statuary in the façade of the new town hall which was an offence to public decency. . . . And if in addition to that you added a soliloquy from your daughter Millicent to the effect that she intended to obtain on credit from your bootmakers, charging them to your account, a pair of scarlet morocco shoes with two-inch heels with which to go joy-riding on the Sunday with a young actor who played under the name of Hildebrand Hare and who had had his portrait in your paper. . . . If you gave all these long speeches one after the other you might be aware of a certain dullness when you reread that *compte rendu*. . . . But if you carefully broke up petunias, statuary, and flower-show motives and put them down in little shreds, one contrasting with the other, you would arrive at something much more coloured, animated, lifelike and interesting, and you would convey a profoundly significant lesson as to the self-engrossment of humanity. Into that live scene you could then drop the piece of news that you wanted to convey and so you would carry the chapter a good many stages forward.

—*—

Here, again, compromise must necessarily come in: there must come a point in the dramatic working up of every scene in which the characters do directly answer each other, for a speech or for two

or three speeches. It was in this department, as
has already been pointed out, that Conrad was
matchless and the writer very deficient. Or, again,
a point may come in which it is necessary — in
which at least it is to take the line of least re-
sistance — to report directly a whole tremendous
effort of eloquence as ebullient as an oration by
Mr. Lloyd George on the hymns of the Welsh
nation. For there are times when the paraphernalia of indirect speech, interruptions, and the rest
retard your action too much. Then they must go;
the sense of reality must stand down before the
necessity to get on.

But, on the whole, the indirect, interrupted
method of handling interviews is invaluable for
giving a sense of the complexity, the tantalisation,
the shimmering, the haze, that life is. In the pre-
War period the English novel began at the beginning of a hero's life and went straight on to his
marriage without pausing to look aside. This was
all very well in its way, but the very great objection could be offered against it that such a story
was too confined to its characters and, too self-
centredly, went on, *in vacuo*. If you are so set on
the affair of your daughter Millicent with the
young actor that you forget that there *are* flower
shows and town halls with nude statuary your in-

tellect will appear a thing much more circumscribed than it should be. Or, to take a larger matter. A great many novelists have treated of the late War in terms solely of the War: in terms of pip squeaks, trench coats, wire aprons, shells, mud, dust, and sending the bayonet home with a grunt. For that reason interest in the late War is said to have died. But, had you taken part actually in those hostilities, you would know how infinitely little part the actual fighting itself took in your mentality. You would be lying on your stomach, in a beast of a funk, with an immense, horrid German barrage going on all over and round you and with hell and all let loose. But, apart from the occasional, petulant question, "When the deuce will our fellows get going and shut 'em up?" your thoughts were really concentrated on something quite distant: on your daughter Millicent's hair, on the fall of the Asquith Ministry, on your financial predicament, on why your regimental ferrets kept on dying, on whether Latin is really necessary to an education. . . . You were there, but great shafts of thought from the outside, distant and unattainable world infinitely for the greater part occupied your mind.

It was that effect, then, that Conrad and the writer sought to get into their work, that being Impressionism.

But these two writers were not unaware that there are other methods; they were not rigid in their own methods; they were sensible to the fact that compromise is at all times necessary in the execution of every work of art.

—*—

Let us come, then, to the eternally vexed seas of the Literary Ocean.

STYLE

We agreed on this axiom:

The first business of Style is to make work interesting: the second business of Style is to make work interesting: the third business of Style is to make work interesting: the fourth business of Style is to make work interesting: the fifth business of Style. . . .

—*—

Style, then, has no other business.

A style interests when it carries the reader along; it is then a good style. A style ceases to interest when by reason of disjointed sentences, over-used words, monotonous or jog-trot cadences, it fatigues the reader's mind. *Too* startling words, however apt, *too* just images, *too* great displays of cleverness are apt in the long run to be as fatiguing as the most over-used words or the most jog-trot cadences. That a face resembles a Dutch clock has been too

often said; to say that it resembles a ham is inexact
and conveys nothing; to say that it has the mourn-
fulness of an old, squashed-in meat tin, cast away
on a waste building lot, would be smart—but too
much of that sort of thing would become a nui-
sance. To say that a face was cramoisy is undesir-
able; few people nowadays know what the word
means. Its employment will make the reader marvel at the user's erudition; in thus marvelling he
ceases to consider the story and an impression of
vagueness or length is produced on his mind. A
succession of impressions of vagueness and length
render a book in the end unbearable.

There are, of course, pieces of writing intended
to convey the sense of the author's cleverness,
knowledge of obsolete words or power of inventing similes: with such exercises Conrad and the
writer never concerned themselves.

We used to say, the first lesson that an author
has to learn is that of humility. Blessed are the
humble because they do not get between the
reader's legs. Before everything the author must
learn to suppress himself; he must learn that the
first thing he has to consider is his story and the
last thing that he has to consider is his story, and
in between that he will consider his story.

We used to say that a passage of good style began with a fresh, usual word, and continued with fresh, usual words to the end; there was nothing more to it. When we felt that we had really got hold of the reader, with a great deal of caution we would introduce a word not common to a very limited vernacular, but that only very occasionally. Very occasionally indeed; practically never. Yet it is in that way that a language grows and keeps alive. People get tired of hearing the same words over and over again. . . . It is again a matter for compromise.

—*—

Our chief masters in style were Flaubert and Maupassant: Flaubert in the greater degree, Maupassant in the less. In about the proportion of a sensible man's whisky and soda. We stood as it were on those hills and thence regarded the world. We remembered long passages of Flaubert; elaborated long passages in his spirit and with his cadences and then translated them into passages of English as simple as the subject under treatment would bear. We remembered short, staccato passages of Maupassant; invented short, staccato passages in his spirit and then translated them into English as simple as the subject would bear. Differing subjects bear differing degrees of simplicity. To apply exactly the same timbre of language to a dreadful interview between a father and a daughter as to the description of a child's bedroom at night is impracticable because it is unnatural. In thinking of the frightful scene with your daughter Millicent which ruined your life, town councillor and parliamentary candidate though you had become, you will find that your mind employs a verbiage quite different from that which occurs when you remember Millicent asleep, her little mouth just slightly opened, her toys beside the shaded night-light.

Our vocabulary, then, was as simple as was practicable. But there are degrees of simplicity. We employed as a rule in writing the language that we employed in talking the one to the other. When we used French in speaking we tried mentally to render in English the least literary equivalent of the phrase. We were, however, apt to employ in our conversation words and periphrases that are not in use by, say, financiers. This was involuntary, we imagining that we talked simply enough. But later a body of younger men with whom the writer spent some years would say, after dinner, "Talk like a book, H. . . . Do talk like a book!" The writer would utter some speeches in the language that he employed when talking with Conrad; but he never could utter

more than a sentence or two at a time. The whole
mess would roar with laughter and, for some
minutes, would render his voice inaudible.

—∗—

If you will reflect on the language you then
employed — and the writer — you will find that it
was something like, "Cheerio, old bean. The
beastly Adjutant's Parade is at five ack emma.
Will you take my Johnnie's and let me get a real
good fug in my downy bug-walk? I'm fair blind
to the wide to-night." That was the current language then and, in the earlier days of our conversations, some equivalent with which we were
unacquainted must normally have prevailed. That
we could hardly have used in our books, since
within a very short time such languages become
incomprehensible. Even to-day the locution "ack
emma" is no longer used and the expression "blind
to the wide" is incomprehensible — the very state
is unfamiliar — to more than half the English-
speaking populations of the globe.

—∗—

So we talked and wrote a Middle-High English
of as unaffected a sort as would express our
thoughts. And that was all that there really was
to our "style." Our greatest admiration for a
stylist in any language was given to W. H. Hudson
of whom Conrad said that his writing was like

the grass that the good God made to grow and when it was there you could not tell how it came.

—*—

Carefully examined, a good — an interesting — style will be found to consist in a constant succession of tiny, unobservable surprises. If you write — "His range of subject was very wide and his conversation very varied and unusual; he could rouse you with his perorations or lull you with his periods; therefore his conversation met with great appreciation and he made several fast friends" — you will not find the world very apt to be engrossed by what you have set down. The results will be different if you put it, "He had the power to charm or frighten rudimentary souls into an aggravated witch-dance; he could also fill the small souls of the pilgrims with bitter misgivings; he had one devoted friend at least, and he had conquered one soul in the world that was neither rudimentary nor tainted with self-seeking."

—*—

Or, let us put the matter in another way. The catalogue of an ironmonger's store is uninteresting as literature because things in it are all classified and thus obvious; the catalogue of a farm sale is more interesting because things in it are contrasted. No one would for long read: Nails, drawn wire, $\frac{1}{2}$ inch, per lb. . . .; nails, do., $\frac{3}{4}$

inch, per lb. . . .; nails, do., inch, per lb. . . .
But it is often not disagreeable to read desultorily:
"*Lot* 267. Pair rabbit gins. *Lot* 268, Antique
powder flask. *Lot* 269, Malay Kris. *Lot* 270, Set
of six sporting prints by Herring. *Lot* 271, Silver
caudle cup . . ." for that, as far as it goes, has the
quality of surprise.

That is, perhaps, enough about Style. This is
not a technical manual, and at about this point
we arrive at a region in which the writer's memory
is not absolutely clear as to the points on which
he and Conrad were agreed. We made in addition an infinite number of experiments, together
and separately, in points of style and cadence.
The writer, as has been said, wrote one immense
book entirely in sentences of not more than ten
syllables. He read the book over. He found it
read immensely long. He went through it all
again. He joined short sentences; he introduced
relative clauses; he wrote in long sentences that
had a gentle sonority and ended with a dying fall.
The book read less long. Much less long.

Conrad also made experiments, but not on such
a great scale since he could always have the benefit of the writer's performances of that sort. The
writer only remembers specifically one instance of

an exercise on Conrad's part. He was interested in blank verse at the moment — though he took no interest in English verse as a rule — and the writer happening to observe that whole passages of "Heart of Darkness" were not very far off blank verse, Conrad tried for a short time to run a paragraph into decasyllabic lines. The writer remembers the paragraph quite well. It is the one which begins:

She walked with measured steps, draped in striped and fringed cloths, treading the earth proudly with a slight jingle and flash of barbarous ornaments. . . .

But he cannot remember what Conrad added or took away. There come back vaguely to him a line or two like:

She carried high her head, her hair was done
In the shape of a helmet; she had greaves of brass
To the knee; gauntlets of brass to th' elbow.
A crimson spot. . . .

That, however, may just as well be the writer's contrivance as Conrad's: it happened too long ago for the memory to be sure. A little later, the writer occupying himself with writing French rhymed *vers libre*, Conrad tried his hand at that too. He produced:

Riez toujours! La vie n'est pas si gaie,
Ces tristes jours quand à travers la haie
Tombe le long rayon
Dernier
De mon soleil qui gagne
Les sommets, la montagne,
De l'horizon. . . .

There was a line or two more that the writer has forgotten.

That was Conrad's solitary attempt to write verse.

—✦—

We may as well put the rest of this matter under a separate heading:

CADENCE

This was the one subject upon which we never came to any agreement. It was the writer's view that every one has a natural cadence of his own from which in the end he cannot escape. Conrad held that a habit of good cadence could be acquired by the study of models. His own he held came to him from constant reading of Flaubert. He did himself probably an injustice.

—✦—

But questions of cadence and accentuation as of prosody in general we were chary of discussing. They were matters as to which Conrad was very touchy. His ear was singularly faulty for one who was a great writer of elaborated prose so that at times the writer used to wonder how the deuce he *did* produce his effects of polyphonic closings to paragraphs. In speaking English he had practically no idea of accentuation whatever, and indeed no particular habits. He would talk of Mr. Cunninghame Graham's book "Success" alternately as "*Suc*cess" and "Suc*cess*" half a dozen times in the course of a conversation about the works of that very wonderful writer. Over French he was not much better. He became quite enraged when told that if the first line of his verse quoted above was to be regarded as decasyllabic— and it *must* by English people be regarded as decasyllabic—then the word *vie* must be a monosyllable in spite of its termination in e. He had in the second line quite correctly allowed for *tristes* as being two syllables, and *tombe* in the third. In the clash of French verse-theories of those days he might be correct or incorrect without committing a solecism, but he could not be incorrect in the first line and formal in the others. Conrad's face would cloud over. He would snatch up a volume of Racine and read half a dozen lines. He would exclaim contemptuously, "Do you mean to say that each of those verses *con*sists of ten syllables?" . . . Yet he would have read the verse impeccably. . . . He would flush up to the eyes. He would cry, " Did you ever hear a Frenchman say 'vee-yeh' when he meant 'vee?' You never did! *Jamais de la vie!*" And with fury he would read his verse aloud, making, with a slight stammer, *vie* a monosyllable and, with impetus, two syllables each out of *tristes* and *tombe*. He would begin to gesticulate, his eyes flashing. . . .

One would change the subject of discussion to the unfailing topic of the rottenness of French as a medium for poetry, finding perfect harmony again in the thought that French was as rotten for verse-poetry as was English for any sort of prose. . . .

The curious thing was that when he read his prose aloud his accentuation was absolutely fault-less. So that it always seemed to the writer that Conrad's marvellous gift of language was, in the end, dramatic. When he talked his sense of pho-netics was dormant, but the moment it came to any kind of performance the excitement would quicken the brain centres that governed his articulation. It was, indeed, the same with his French. When conversing desultorily with the writer, he had much of the accent and the negligence of an aristocratic, meridional lounger of the seventies. . . . But when at Lamb House, Rye, he addressed

compliments to Mr. Henry James, you could imagine, if you closed your eyes, that it was the senior actor of the Théâtre Français, addressing an
eulogium to the bust of Molière. . . .

—✳—

Probably the mere thought of reading aloud
subconsciously aroused memories of once-heard
orations of Mr. Gladstone or John Bright; so, in
writing, even to himself he would accentuate and
pronounce his words as had done those now long-
defunct orators. . . . And it is to be remembered
that during all those years the writer wrote every
word that he wrote with the idea of reading aloud
to Conrad, and that during all those years Conrad
wrote what he wrote with the idea of reading it
aloud to this writer.

STRUCTURE

That gets rid, as far as is necessary in order to
give a pretty fair idea of Conrad's methods, of
the questions that concern the texture of a book.
More official or more learned writers who shall
not be novelists shall treat of this author's prose
with less lightness — but assuredly too with less
love. . . . Questions then of vocabulary, selection
of incident, style, cadence and the rest concern
themselves with the colour and texture of prose
and, since this writer, again, will leave to more

suitable pens the profounder appraisements of Conrad's morality, philosophy and the rest, there remains only to say a word or two on the subject of form.

—*—

Conrad, then, never wrote a true short story, a matter of two or three pages of minutely considered words, ending with a smack . . . with what the French call a *coup de canon*. His stories were always what for lack of a better phrase one has to call "long-short" stories. For these the form is practically the same as that of the novel. Or, to avoid the implication of saying that there is only one form for the novel, it would be better to put it that the form of long-short stories may vary as much as may the form for novels. The short story of Maupassant, of Tchekhov or even of the late O. Henry is practically stereotyped — the introduction of a character in a word or two, a word or two for atmosphere, a few paragraphs for story, and then, click! a sharp sentence that flashes the illumination of the idea over the whole.

—*—

This Conrad — and for the matter of that, the writer — never so much as attempted, either apart or in collaboration. The reason for this lies in all that is behind the mystic word "justification." Before everything a story must convey a sense of inevitability: that which happens in it must seem to be the only thing that could have happened. Of course a character may cry, "If I had then acted differently how different everything would now be." The problem of the author is to make his then action the only action that character could have taken. It must be inevitable, because of his character, because of his ancestry, because of past illness or on account of the gradual coming together of the thousand small circumstances by which Destiny, who is inscrutable and august, will push us into one certain predicament. Let us illustrate:

In rendering your long friendship with, and ultimate bitter hostility towards, your neighbour Mr. Slack, who had a greenhouse painted with Cox's aluminum paint, you will, if you wish to get yourself in with the scrupulousness of a Conrad, have to provide yourself, in the first place, with an ancestry at least as far back as your grandparents. To account for your own stability of character and physical robustness you will have to give yourself two dear old grandparents in a lodge at the gates of a great nobleman: if necessary you will have to give them a brightly polished copper kettle simmering on a spotless hob, with silhouettes on each side of the mantel: in order to account for the lamentable procedure of your daughter Millicent you must provide yourself with an actress or gipsy-grandmother. Or at least with a French one. This grandmother will have lived, unfortunately unmarried, with some one of eloquence — possibly with the great Earl-Prime Minister at whose gates is situated the humble abode of your other grandparents — at any rate she will have lived with some one from whom you will have inherited your eloquence. From her will have descended the artistic gifts to which the reader will owe your admirable autobiographic novel.

If you have any physical weakness, to counterbalance the robustness of your other grandparents, you will provide your mother, shortly before your birth, with an attack of typhoid fever, due to a visit to Venice in company with your father, who was a gentleman's courier in the family in which your mother was a lady's maid. Your father, in order to be a courier, will have had, owing to his illegitimacy, to live abroad in very poor circumstances. The very poor circumstances will illustrate the avarice of his statesman father — an avarice which will have descended to you in the shape of that carefulness in money matters that, reacting on the detrimental tendencies inherited by Millicent from her actress-grandmother, so lamentably influences your daughter's destiny.

And of course there will have to be a great deal more than that, always supposing you to be as scrupulous as was Conrad in this matter of justification. For Conrad — and for the matter of that the writer — was never satisfied that he had really and sufficiently got his characters in; he was never convinced that he had convinced the reader; this accounting for the great lengths of some of his books. He never introduced a character, however subsidiary, without providing that character with ancestry and hereditary characteristics, or at least with home surroundings — always supposing that character had any influence on the inevitability of the story. Any policeman who arrested any character must be "justified", because the manner in which he effected the arrest, his mannerisms, his vocabulary and his voice, might have a permanent effect on the psychology of the prisoner. The writer remembers Conrad using almost those very words during the discussion of the plot of "The Secret Agent."

This method, unless it is very carefully handled, is apt to have the grave defect of holding a story back very considerably. You must as a rule bring the biography of a character in only after you have introduced the character; yet, if you introduce a policeman to make an arrest the rendering of his biography might well retard the action of an exciting point in the story. . . . It becomes then your job to arrange that the very arresting of the action is an incitement of interest in the reader, just as, if you serialise a novel, you take care to let the words "*to be continued in our next*" come in at as harrowing a moment as you can contrive.

And of course the introducing of the biography of a character may have the great use of giving contrast to the tone of the rest of the book. . . . Supposing that in your history of your affair with Mr. Slack you think that the note of your orderly middle-class home is growing a little monotonous, it would be very handy if you could discover that Mr. Slack had a secret, dipsomaniacal wife, confined in a country cottage under the care of a rather criminal old couple; with a few pages of biography of that old couple you could give a very pleasant relief to the sameness of your narrative. In that way the sense of reality is procured.

PHILOSOPHY, ETC.

We agreed that the novel is absolutely the only vehicle for the thought of our day. With the novel you can do anything: you can inquire into every department of life, you can explore every department of the world of thought. The one thing that you can not do is to propagandise, as author, for any cause. You must not, as author, utter any views; above all, you must not fake any events. You must not, however humanitarian you may be, over-elaborate the fear felt by a coursed rabbit.

—*—

It is obviously best if you can contrive to be without views at all; your business with the world is rendering, not alteration. You have to render life with such exactitude that more specialised beings than you, learning from you what are the secret needs of humanity, may judge how many white-tiled bathrooms are, or to what extent parliamentary representation is, necessary for the happiness of men and women. If, however, your yearning to amend the human race is so great that you cannot possibly keep your fingers out of the watch-springs there is a device that you can adopt.

—*—

Let us suppose that you feel tremendously strong views as to sexual immorality or temperance. You feel that you must express these, yet you know that like, say, M. Anatole France, who is also a propagandist, you are a supreme novelist. You must then invent, justify and set going in your novel a character who can convincingly express your views. If you are a gentleman you will also invent, justify and set going characters to express views opposite to those you hold. . . .

※

You have reached the climax of your long relationship with Mr. Slack; you are just going to address a deputation that has come to invite you to represent your native city in the legislature of your country. The deputation is just due. Five minutes before it arrives to present you with the proudest emotion of your life, you learn that your daughter Millicent is going to have a child by Mr. Slack. (Him, of course, you will have already "justified" as the likely seducer of a young lady whose cupidity in the matter of bangles and shoes you, by your pecuniary carefulness, have kept perpetually on the stretch.) Mr. Slack has a dipsomaniac wife so there is no chance of his making the matter good. . . .

You thus have an admirable opportunity of expressing with emphasis quite a number of views through the mouth of the character whom you have so carefully "justified" as yourself. Quite a number of views!

※

That then was, cursorily stated, the technique that we evolved at the Pent. It will be found to be nowadays pretty generally accepted as the normal way of handling the novel. It is founded on common sense and some of its maxims may therefore stand permanently. Or they may not.

PROGRESSION D'EFFET

There is just one other point. In writing a novel we agreed that every word set on paper— *every* word set on paper— must carry the story forward and that, as the story progressed, the story must be carried forward faster and faster and with more and more intensity. That is called *progression d'effet,* words for which there is no English equivalent.

One might go on to further technicalities, such as how to squeeze the last drop out of a subject. The writer has, however, given an instance of this in describing how we piled perils of the hangman's rope on the unfortunate John Kemp. To go deeper into the matter would be to be too technical. Besides enough has been said in this chapter to show you what was the character, the scrupulousness and the common sense of our hero.

There remains to add once more:

But these two writers were not unaware—were not unaware—*that there are other methods of writing novels. They were not rigid even in their own methods. They were sensible to the fact that*

compromise is at all times necessary to the execu-
tion of a work of art.

The lay reader will be astonished at this repetition and at these italics. They are inserted for the
benefit of gentlemen and ladies who comment on
books in the Press.

LANGUAGE

It would be disingenuous to avoid the subject
of language. This is the only matter on which the
writer ever differed fundamentally from Conrad.
It was one upon which the writer felt so deeply
that, for several years, he avoided his friend's
society. The pain of approaching the question is
thus very great.

Conrad's dislike for the English language, then,
was, during all the years of our association, extreme,
his contempt for his medium unrivalled. Again
and again during the writing of, say, "Nostromo"
he expressed passionate regret that it was then too
late to hope to make a living by writing in French,
and as late as 1916 he expressed to the writer an
almost equally passionate envy of the writer who
was in a position to write in French, propaganda
for the government of the French Republic. . . .
And Conrad's contempt for English as a prose
language was not, as in the writer's case, mitigated

by love for English as the language for verse-
poetry. For, to the writer, English is as much
superior to French in the one particular as French
to English in the other.

–✳–

Conrad, however, knew nothing of, and cared
less for, English verse — and his hatred for English as a prose medium reached such terrible
heights that during the writing of "Nostromo"
the continual weight of Conrad's depression broke
the writer down. We had then published "Romance" and Conrad, breaking, in the interests of
that work, his eremitic habits, decided that we
ought to show ourselves in Town. The writer
therefore took a very large, absurd house on Campden Hill and proceeded to "entertain." Conrad
had lodgings also on Campden Hill. At this time
"Nostromo" had begun to run as a serial in a very
popular journal, and on the placards of that journal Conrad's name appeared on every hoarding in
London. This publicity caused Conrad an un-
believable agony, he conceiving himself for ever
dishonoured by such vicarious pandering to popularity.

–✳–

It was the most terrible period of Conrad's life
and of the writer's. Conrad at that time considered himself completely unsuccessful; ignored

by the public; ill-treated by the critics (he was certainly at that date being treated with unusual stupidity by the critics) ; he was convinced that he would never make a decent living. And he was convinced that he would never master English. He used to declare that English was a language in which it was impossible to write a direct statement. That was true enough. He used to declare that to make a direct statement in English is like trying to kill a mosquito with a forty-foot stock whip when you have never before handled a stock whip. One evening he made, in French, to the writer, the impassioned declaration which will be found in French at the end of this volume. On the following afternoon he made a terrible scene at the writer's house. . . .

The writer was at the time very much harassed. The expense of keeping up a rather portentous establishment made it absolutely necessary that he should add considerably to his income with his pen — a predicament with which he had not yet been faced. There was nothing in that except that it was almost impossible to find time to write. An epidemic of influenza running through the house crippled its domestic staff so that all sorts of household tasks had of necessity to be performed by the writer: there were, in addition,

social duties—and the absolute necessity of carrying Conrad every afternoon through a certain
quantum of work without which he must miss his
weekly instalments in the popular journal. . . .

—⋆—

At an At Home there, amongst eminently de-
corous people, a well-meaning but unfortunate
gentleman congratulated Conrad on the fact that
his name appeared on all the hoardings and Conrad considered that these congratulations were
ironical gibes at him because his desperate circumstances had forced him to agree to the dis-
honour of serialisation in a popular journal. . . .

—⋆—

Conrad's indictment of the English language
was this, that no English word is a word; that
all English words are instruments for exciting
blurred emotions. "Oaken" in French means
"made of oak wood"—nothing more. "Oaken"
in English connotes innumerable moral attributes:
it will connote stolidity, resolution, honesty, blond
features, relative unbreakableness, absolute un-
bendableness—also, made of oak. . . . The con-
sequence is that no English word has clean edges:
a reader is always, for a fraction of a second, un-
certain as to which meaning of the word the writer
intends. Thus, all English prose is blurred. Conrad desired to write prose of extreme limpidity. . . .

We may let it go at that. In later years Conrad achieved a certain fluency and a great limpidity of language. He then regretted that for him all the romance of writing was gone — the result being "The Rover", which strikes the writer as being a very serene and beautiful work. . . . In between the two he made tributes to the glory of the English language, by implication contemning the tongue that Flaubert used. This struck the writer, at that time in a state of exhausted depression, as unforgivable — as the very betrayal of Dain by Tom Lingard. . . . Perhaps it was. If it were Conrad faced the fact in that book. There are predicaments that beset great Adventurers, in dark hours, in the shallows: the overtired nerve will fail. . . . We may well let it go at that. . . .

—*—

"*For it would be delightful to catch the echo of the desperate and funny quarrels that enlivened these old days. The pity of it is that there comes a time when all the fun of one's life must be looked for in the past. . . .*"

—*—

Those were Conrad's last words on all the matters of our collaborations here treated of. They were, too, almost his last words. . . . For those who can catch them here, then, are the echoes. . . .

Part IV

THAT, TOO, IS ROMANCE . . .

WITH the turn of the century we took up again "Romance."

➤

For a long time we had talked of going to Bruges in order to get quiet in which to finish this work; this not because the Pent was noisy, but its corners seemed to be filled with the whispering echoes of our struggles. The crux of the difficulties in this book had arrived. By that time a great deal of it was finished and in about its present condition.

➤

Conrad's allotment of the authorship of the parts of this work had better be given here again.

"I suppose our recollections agree," he writes to the author. "Mine in their simplest form, are:

"First part, yours; Second part, mainly yours, with a little by me on points of seamanship and suchlike small matters; Third part about 60 per cent. mine with important touches by you. Fourth part mine, with here and there an important sentence by you: Fifth part practically all yours, including the famous sentence at which we both

exclaimed: 'This is Genius' (Do you remember
what it was?) with perhaps half a dozen lines by
me."

⸻

The writer's recollection agrees except as to the
Fourth part, which does not contain one word by
the writer. How that came about shall now be
recounted.

⸻

The writer with his family and paraphernalia
had transported themselves to Bruges to await
Conrad and his. Bruges is a grey, silent town with
crowstep gables to the house fronts, its shadows
being shot with the gleams from canals that run
through the streets. Its roof-level is dominated by
an immense belfry from which there descend
chimes. The chimes are practically never silent.
Beautifully and drowsily five minutes before every
quarter of the hour they begin to announce that the
quarter is about to strike; for ten minutes after
the quarter has struck they go on announcing that the
quarter has struck. The hour is greeted for a quarter
of an hour by chimes that announce that the hour
is about to strike; for forty-five minutes after the
hour has struck they continue to announce that the
hour has struck. The hours and the quarters are
struck on great bells whose overtones go on rever-
berating for fifty and for ten minutes respectively.

. . . That is impressionism: the impressionism of those who in Bruges lie awake at night. There are in Bruges a great number of churches — all with bells — and some very lovely, bright little pictures by Van Eyck. There was also an English pension to which we had agreed to go. Conrad liked to be amongst English people when abroad. . . . Bruges is also very relaxing: except at night it is difficult not to sleep.

—

The Contents page of "Romance" looks like this:

PART FIRST
THE QUARRY AND THE BEACH

PART SECOND
THE GIRL WITH THE LIZARD

PART THIRD
CASA RIEGO

PART FOURTH
BLADE AND GUITAR

PART FIFTH
THE LOT OF MAN

. . . whose names are five sweet symphonies in the *capa y espada* manner. They are all Conrad's, those names. There was nothing he loved so much as inventing titles for Parts: it was like

being a herald proclaiming war from the steps of
St. Paul's. . . .

On arrival in Bruges the author was carrying
the manuscript of Parts One, Two and Three complete. The end of the book was also done by
then, exactly as it stands, except for the peroration
over which, subsequently, we worked for twenty
hours on end. We were to meet, cheered by the
new atmosphere of Bruges and, in a rush, finish
off Part Four and the opening of Part Five. . . .
In three or four days. Then we would take a
week's holiday and look at the churches. We had
also planned an excursion to Ghent: two sailors
ashore after a four years' voyage. For, by that
time, we had been, on and off, four years over
" Romance."

So there we were in Bruges, in the English
pension, waiting for Conrad. The English pension seemed to be distinguished chiefly by brown
linoleum, bentwood chairs in long perspectives,
long teeth in withered faces, dimness and placards
forbidding you to take water between certain hours
from certain taps — and by complete, absolute, un-
shakable lassitude. There was no place in which
to write. When, with a desperate struggle of the
will, the writer took a private sitting room on the

ground floor, little boys from the school opposite used to throw in at the windows envelopes full of ink which made a delectable mess. About the shadowy streets and along the dim canals the Briton was pursued by crowds of little boys whose shouts of *Vivent les Boers!* gave temporary animation to Bruges la Morte.

—✶—

Conrad delayed to come . . . "Romance" was thus hung up. We had agreed that the writer would work in the mornings on "Romance" whilst Conrad wrote—probably "Typhoon"—at the same time. We would play dominoes in agreeable cafés during the afternoons and after dinner collaborate gaily. The work would take only a few days. . . .

—✶—

It was impossible to do anything during the day in Bruges but lie on one's bed; at night it was impossible to sleep for chimes and mosquitoes. . . . Conrad delayed to come. . . . The diet of the English pension — thin slices of cold mutton, potatoes boiled in water, "greens" boiled in water which remained with the greens — began seriously to deteriorate a digestion used to food more elaborate. The taste of the greens was never out of the mouth. . . . We hesitated to change our lodging because Conrad was coming to-morrow.

He liked to be amongst English people when abroad. It was perhaps "To-morrow" that he was then writing, or both "To-morrow" and "Typhoon." The withered faces and the long teeth that phantasmally loomed in the more dim places of the English pension were curious to know why we needed a private sitting room. . . . To write a book in? . . . A novel? Oh, good gracious. . . . They had never been in a pension with a novelist before. . . . Was it quite. . . . Of course you locked your door at night. . . . But they had always thought. . . . Like common soldiers, you know. . . . Not allowed in the best. . . .

—✳—

Telegrams went back and forth between the pension and the Pent. . . . "Book just being finished," came the cheerful news from the Pent. Pinker would come down with large sum. . . . The early summer waned; the dog-days were intolerable there. . . . The French-Swiss governess, indispensable, declared she would not stop another day in Bruges. . . . Little boys calling her *Sale Anglaise* had thrown ink over her pink-striped, best dimity dress. . . . Agitated packings began. In the midst of them a telegram from Sandling Junction to say, "Starting."

—✳—

There was, of course, a rush to Ostend where

the boat comes in. Travellers not coming by boat are not allowed on the Ostend-Bruges Express. The writer visited the *sous chef de gare: Statie-Onderovoorste.* He removed his hat, bowing with exquisite politeness, and announced to a uniformed man as big as a sea-lion "*qu'il serait infiniment reconnaissant si M. Le Chef de Gare lui accorderait la permission. . . .*" The sea-lion mumbled, "*Wat wolt gi? . . .* Wadger want?" The writer wanted permission to travel by the Ostend-Bruges Express. The sea-lion waved a flapper and cried: "Vat do *I* kerr? . . . Do wadger want. . . . Ko er-way. . . ."

—

Conrad appeared on the platform, overburdened by the weight of a large-small boy, not very well. . . . Bearers staggering after that Congo caravan. . . . The scared face of Amy Foster, maid, who had never been abroad. . . . A swarm of frightened ticket collectors running alongside. Conrad infuriated. . . . The caravan is assimilated by the express. . . . The timid ticket collectors waver round the open door of the carriage bleating, "Tickets, pliss. Billets. *Koupangs. . . . Bitte die Fahrkarten. . . .* " Conrad, exhausted but volanic, sunk on the cushions, exclaims, "Dirt: foreigners. . . . *Sales Belges.* . . . Damn, damn, *damn! . . .*" The sea-lion in an unbuttoned blue tunic with gilt buttons — a tunic large enough to be a truck cover — waddles like a great sow amongst a poultry yard of ticket collectors. He exclaims, "*Det maakt mix. . . . Verrokter Engelsker . . .* Ko away. . . ." The ticket collectors disperse. . . . Whether Conrad had any tickets the writer never knew. He certainly never showed them. . . . It is perhaps in that way that one *ought* to handle foreigners. . . .

Conrad remained wrapped in a comminative gloom, the train going over the flat lands. He contrived to communicate to the milder writer that all . . . all . . . all these things: the train, the boat, the mislaid trunks, the ticket collectors and the whole dreary waste of foreigners were *his* — the writer's — fault. . . . One ought to be English. . . . The writer ought to be English. . . . Why wasn't he English to the soul? Asking permission of a *Statie-Onderovoorste!* . . . It made these fellows not know their places. . . . But it would be all right when we got to the English pension, amongst English people. . . .

At the first sight of the first placard on the first landing, surrounded by long teeth that peeped from the gloom of corridors, Conrad stiffened, like a sudden corpse.

WATER MUST NOT BE DRAWN FROM THIS TAP
BETWEEN THE HOURS OF ELEVEN AND TEN MORN-
ING OR EVENING. GUESTS WILL BE STRICTLY SILENT
ON THE STAIRS. A FINE OF ONE FRANC TWENTY-
FIVE WILL BE ENACTED FOR EVERY FIVE MINUTES
LATE AT MEALS. NO SMOKING IN THE DINING-
ROOM SALONS STAIRS BATH ROOMS OR W.C.S. BOOTS
ARE NOT CLEANED IN THE CORRIDORS. ANGLICAN
SERVICE DAILY IN THE DINING-ROOM FROM NINE
THIRTY TO ONE. . . .

Thus England spoke.

What Conrad said made all the glimmering
teeth vanish from those corridors for the next seven
hours. He disappeared. Gone.

He seemed to be gone for days. . . . But within
seven hours we were all aboard the tram for
Knocke. . . . He had met an admirable Abbé in
the Place du Beffroi. . . . He had been directed
to that seashore. Admirable hotel. . . . Wonderful domino players. . . . Charming Dutch,
French, Spanish, German fellow guests. . . . Belgians not so bad. . . . Best class. . . . Director
of Brussels orchestra. . . . Wagnerian cantatrice.
. . . Unsurpassed sands. . . . Cooking . . . Hum,
hum. . . . Four francs a day bath and *vin com-
pris.* . . . A little music with the *chasse café, mon*

vieux. . . . We will finish "Romance" in a
week. . . .

—✳—

It was not so bad. When Conrad really went
at it he fell on his feet all right. . . . Knocke
was just within the Belgian border. You could
run in a sand-yacht in front of the dunes, right
to Sluys, far in Holland. . . . The hotel was very
airy, the fellow guests were pleasant. You could
play in domino or *écarté* tournaments or sand-
tennis ones. Even Miss Benny van der Meer de
Walcheren was charming when, at meals, her
voice was not shaking the glasses on the trays in
the sixth-floor back bedroom where we tried to
collaborate. . . .

—✳—

Alas! A child fell ill; the book would not go
in the mornings in the top room; "Romance" in
the mornings would not go, either, on the corner
of the café table: doctors had to be fetched at
midnights in the teeth of westerly gales, the foam
white like a bar across the sky, the sand skinning
your lips. The child was very ill. . . . The
writer developed symptoms of idiocy never before
suspected. . . . Owing to the illness of the child
it was impossible for Conrad to invent the escape
of John Kemp from the Casa Riego in Rio Media.
The writer was set to invent. . . . He invented

John Kemp boarding the *Lion*, or some other ship, with the fainting Seraphina on one arm: Kemp swarming up a rope with his burden and shooting two negroes whose white teeth gleamed at the wheel. . . . It became touch and go with the child. Conrad had very bad gout, his wrist all wapped up. He groaned all day long in the top room. Writing was impossible. From time to time he would smile distractedly to the writer and say, "If I didn't know that you, *mon vieux*, were writing away at that book I should go mad. . . ."

—*—

Alas! . . . In the café downstairs the sand and the draughts filtered round the writer's ankles. The ink was full of sand, the typewriter was stopped by sand, the marble table on which one wrote was like ice. Autumn was there; the voice of Miss Benny competed with great gales off the leaden North Sea. . . . The child lived to become an admirable son, and to make the proudest of fathers that Conrad was, the discreetly proudest of grandfathers. . . . So Conrad had mind enough to read how the bodies of those white-teethed niggers falling on the wheel made the pirate ship come about, and how John Kemp exclaimed to the villainous O'Brien, "Foiled! And by a stripling!" . . . It was not really as bad as that; but that was how it felt as the writer sat by with Conrad read-

ing the manuscript. Conrad had too bad a head-
ache, and was too bad with the gout to be read to
in the top room that contained a deal table, an
unmade-up bed, some ash trays and a portrait of
Leopold, King of the Belgians, hanging on the
wall askew. . . . Leopold had his revenge for
"The Inheritors" as he simpered down over his
preposterous beard — the ugly Jew! . . .

The writer almost turned. Not because Conrad
did not like John Kemp's pistol practice, but because Conrad's belief in the writer's omniscience
should have put him to the job of writing sea adventures, which was trying him altogether too
high. For Conrad really had that belief; that is
the one certainty that the writer has as to how
Conrad really regarded him. He may have had
affection for the writer or he may not; he may
have had admiration for his gifts or he may not.
The one thing certain is that he really regarded
him as omniscient. Otherwise he would never
have put him at the jobs that he did put him at.
For of our establishment the writer was Bill the
Lizard. It was, "Here Bill. . . . Where's Bill?
. . . Bill, the master says that you've got to go up
the chimney!" all day long. . . . And proud, too!
The writer would have to supply authentic information about Anarchists as about Cabinet Min-

isters, about Courts of Justice as about the emotions of women, about leases, mining shares, brands
of cigarettes, the verse of Christina Rossetti. . . .
He did, too, and was mostly treated with an ex-
aggerated politeness. As to the accusation of omniscience and the politeness there is documentary
evidence: you may read in the preface of "The
Secret Agent" of "the omniscient friend who first
gave me the first suggestion of the book." Or
again — this is Conrad giving you the writer:

The subject of "The Secret Agent" — I mean
the tale — came to me in the shape of a few words
uttered by a friend, in a casual conversation about
anarchists or rather anarchists' activities; how
brought about I do not remember now. . . .

I remember, however, remarking on the criminal futility of the whole thing, doctrine, action,
mentality. . . . Presently . . . we recalled the
already old story of the attempt to blow up Green-
wich Observatory. . . . That outrage could not
be laid hold of mentally in any sort of a way. . . .

I pointed all this out to my friend who remained
silent for a while, and then remarked in his char-
acteristically casual and omniscient manner: "Oh,
that fellow was half an idiot. His sister committed
suicide afterwards." . . . It never occurred to me
later to ask how he arrived at his knowledge. I
am sure that if he had once in his life seen the back
of an anarchist, that must have been the whole of
his connection with the underworld. . . .

That passage is curiously characteristic Conrad.
. . . For what the writer really did say to Conrad
was, "Oh, that fellow was half an idiot! His
sister murdered her husband afterwards and was
allowed to escape by the police. I remember the
funeral. . . ." The suicide was invented by Conrad. And the writer knew — and Conrad knew
that the writer knew — a great many anarchists of
the Goodge Street group, as well as a great many
of the police who watched them. The writer had
provided Conrad with anarchist literature, with
memoirs, with introductions to at least one anarchist young lady who figures in "The Secret Agent."
Indeed, the writer's first poems were set up by that
very young lady on an anarchist printing press.

Acquiring such knowledge is the diversion of
most youths, the writer having once been young.
There are few English boys of spirit who have not
at one time or other dressed up in sweaters and,
with handkerchiefs round their necks, gone after
experience amongst the cutthroats at Wapping
Old Stairs. . . . But Conrad, when he met the
writer after the publication of "The Secret Agent"
with preface in 1920, remarked almost at once and
solicitously:

"You know. . . . The preface to 'The Secret
Agent.' . . . I did not give you away too much.

. . . I was very cautious." . . . He had wished
politely to throw a veil of eternal respectability
over the writer. And he had been afraid that the
suggestion that the writer had once known some
anarchists, thirty-five years before, might ruin the
writer's career! . . . And of course few men in
self-revelations and prefaces have ever so contrived under an aspect of lucidity to throw over
themselves veils of confusion.

For the sake of completing the picture of col-
laborators at work, whilst we are quoting, the
writer will quote here a passage from Stephen
Crane that has always pleased the writer very
much. "You must not be offended," he writes to
some one, "by Hueffer's manner. He patronises
Mr. James, he patronises Mr. Conrad. Of course
he patronises me, and he will patronise Almighty
God when they meet, but God will get used to it,
for Hueffer is all right." With the additional information that it was according to Conrad that
Henry James always referred to the writer as *votre
ami, le jeune homme modeste*, the writer will leave
the reader to make what he can of it. Relationships are extraordinarily indefinable things.

But with the Fourth Part of "Romance" the
writer really did momentarily feel that he was being

tried too high. And he protested. He pointed out
that he knew nothing about the sea, except that it
was salt and bitter. He ought not to have been
set to contrive the escape of John Kemp by sea.
He could have done it overland, and would have
made Kemp just as hangable.

⟶*⟵

Conrad grumbled rather suspiciously that the
writer had managed all right with the pirate attack on the *Breeze* in Part II. The writer pointed
out that it was one thing to elaborate a scene from
the evidence of a trial and to write: "a quarter of
a mile astern and between the land and us, a little
schooner, rather low in the water, curtsying under
a cloud of white canvas—a wonderful thing to
look at." Any one who could describe a pint pot
could write that. But with the impression that
the writer knew all about his, Conrad's past, at the
back of his mind, Conrad said, still suspiciously,
"That's all right. . . . What's the matter with
it? . . ." The implication being that the writer
really knew all about seafaring and had just not
tried when he invented those niggers at the wheel.

⟶*⟵

. . . The fact was that Conrad suspected the
writer of not having taken trouble with the passage,
because of going joy-riding with Miss Benny on a
sand-yacht into Holland. Something like that. . . .

In any case, that was the end of the writer's invention of parts of "Romance." Conrad took over the Fourth Part which begins, "There was a slight, almost imperceptible jar, a faint grating noise, a whispering sound of sand — and the boat, without a splash, floated." In the literature of romantic adventure there is nothing more admirable — unless only, Conrad would have added, "The Purple Land."

So the writer failed Conrad as any other King Tom always fails any Malay Prince, for the labours Conrad put into that immense wad out of the book must have been agonising, and in that matter the writer was past help. . . .

But it must not be imagined that that ended our labours. The Parts once joined up, we went right over the book again, working upon every passage with microscopes. It then went to the printers and there was an interval. But the proof corrections we made were so overwhelming that when we were halfway through the Second Part, Messrs. Smith and Elder sent the manuscript back, suggesting that we might as well make our corrections on that. We went through it all again and, even after that, corrected elaborately. On the last section of the proof we worked at the Pent from ten in the morning till fire-lighting time of the next morning. What our labours amounted to was what follows. This passage from the end of "Romance" has been printed elsewhere as well. The reader may not have seen that book. We worked all that day on those passages, putting in sentences and taking them out; there was a great deal more Conrad at one time, a great deal more Hueffer at another. It all went but what here is given. We were, you see, shortening, shortening, shortening—for the sake of *progression d'effet*.

Part V

THE END

*It takes long enough to realise that some one is
dead at a distance. I had done that. But how
long, how long it needs to know that the life of
your heart has come back from the dead.* For
years afterwards I could not bear to have her out
of my sight.

Of our first meeting in London all I can remember is a speechlessness that was like the awed
hesitation of our overtried souls before the greatness of a change from the verge of despair to the
opening of a supreme joy. The whole world, the
whole of life, with her return had changed all
around me; it enveloped me, it enfolded me so
lightly as not to be felt, so suddenly as not to be
believed in, so completely that that whole meeting
was an embrace, so softly that at last it lapsed into
a sense of rest that was like the fall of a beneficent
and welcome death.

For suffering is the lot of man, but not inevitable failure or worthless despair which is without
end — suffering, the mark of manhood, which
bears within its pain a hope of felicity like a jewel
set in iron. . . .

Her first words were:

"You broke our compact. You went away from
me whilst I was sleeping." Only the deepness of
her reproach revealed the depth of her love, and

the suffering she too had endured to reach a union that was to be without end—and to forgive.

And, looking back, we see Romance—that subtle thing that is mirage—that is life. It is the goodness of the years we have lived through, of the old time when we did this or that, when we dwelt here or there. Looking back it seems a wonderful enough thing that I who am this and she who is that, commencing so far away a life that, after such sufferings borne together and apart, ended so tranquilly there in a world so stable—that she and I should have passed through so much, good chance and evil chance, sad hours and joyful, all lived down and swept away into the little heap of dust that is life. That, too, is Romance.

L'ENVOI

The writer has always considered that that man may be said to have lived happily who has a happy death. What are all the glories of Napoleon as set against his fretted and fretful end? Death is no doubt to all kind; a dulling of the faculties sets in and it is, however fast, a gradual, restful affair. But how kind must death be to the faithful worker, who, having toiled all his life, can say with his last breath, I have achieved. His last backward glance must show all his reverses as mere reverses; but all his progresses have had such permanence as is vouchsafed to us mortals.

So the writer in these sad months and years has one certain happiness. . . .

━━━✴━━━

In the days here mostly treated of, Conrad had a very dreadful, a very agonising life. Few men can so much have suffered; there was about all his depressed moments a note of pain — of agony indeed — that coloured our whole relationship; that caused one to have an almost constant quality of solicitude. It is all very well to say that he had his marvellous resilience. He had, and that was his greatness. But the note of a sailor's life cannot be called preponderantly cheerful whose whole existence is passed in a series of ninety-day passages, in labouring ships, beneath appalling weathers, amongst duties and work too heavy, in continual discomfort and acute physical pain — with, in between each voyage, a few days spent as Jack-ashore. And that, in effect, was the life of Conrad.

━━━✴━━━

His resilience was his own; his oppressions were the work of humanity or of destiny. That is why his personality struck so strong a note of humour. The personality of Conrad as it remains uppermost in the reader's mind was three-fold, with very marked divisions. There was the Conrad with the sharp, agonising intake of the breath who feared your approach because you might jar his gout-martyrised wrist, or the approach of fate with the sharp pain of new disaster. There was the gloomy aristocrat—as man and as intellect—who mused unceasingly upon the treacheries, the muddles, the lack of imagination, the imbecilities which make up the conduct of human affairs; who said after the relation of each new story of incapacity and cruelness: "*Cela vous donne une fière idée de l'homme.*" . . . But most marked in the writer's mind was the alert, dark, extremely polished and tyrannous personality, tremendously awake, tremendously interested in small things, peering through his monocle at something close to the ground, taking in a characteristic and laughing consumedly—at a laborious child progressing engrossedly over a sloping lawn, at a bell-push that functioned of itself in the doorpost of a gentleman who had written about an invisible man—or at the phrase: "Excellency, a few goats. . . ."

Once the writer, in one of his more gorgeous frames of mind, was standing outside his bank, wearing a dazzling *huit-reflets*, a long-tailed morning coat, beautiful trousers and spats, a very high collar that was like enamel, a black satin stock, and dangling a clouded cane. . . . Just like that!

Bored stiff! Thinking nothing at all he gazed down Pall Mall. . . . There approached him an old, shrunken, wizened man, in an unbrushed bowler, an ancient burst-seamed overcoat, one wrist wrapped in flannel, the other hand helping him to lean on a hazel walking stick, cut from a hedge and prepared at home. It had in one tortured eye a round piece of dirty window glass. It said, "*Ford* . . ." "How dare . . ." The writer said to himself, "this atrocious old usurer. . . ." For naturally, no one but a moneylender would have dared . . . in such a get-up.

—⋆—

But, within three minutes, as he stood and talked, the bowler hat was jetty black, the overcoat just come from Poole's, the beard torpedo-shaped, black, and defiant, the confident accents dusky and caressing; the monocle sparkled like cut crystal, the eyes glowed. And, almost more wonderfully, Pall Mall became alive as we went towards the Bodega; it became alive as towns of the true belief awaken in the presence of the Prince of True Believers, come to saunter through his slave market. . . . That, too, was Romance. . . .

—⋆—

But, indeed, with Conrad in it, London was another place. The writer knows his London, has written about it silly books that have been violently if undeservedly belauded; there is not much that you could tell him about what lies two miles or so west of Piccadilly and no one should go anywhere else — at any rate, not in that frame of mind. But with Conrad at your elbow it became extraordinarily altered and more vivid. It was not, of course, that he discoursed archæologies or told you what famous men had lived in such a house in Panton Street. It was simply that he looked at a house front and laughed; or at a hat on a cabman, or his horse, or a tree in a London square, or the skirt of a girl with a bandbox, crossing the road in front of the Ritz, or at the Foreign Office façade. . . . Once we were sitting in the front row of the stalls at the Empire — and Conrad was never tired of wondering at the changes that had come over places of musical entertainment since his time, when they had lodged in cellars, with sanded floors, pots of beer and chairmen. On that night at the Empire there was at least one clergyman with a number of women; ladies is meant. . . . And, during applause by the audience of some *too* middle-class joke, one of us leaned over towards the other and said, "Doesn't one feel lonely in this beastly country!" . . . Which of us it was that spoke neither remembered after, the other had been at that moment thinking so exactly the same thing.

And that must not be taken as want of patriotism to Great Britain on the part of either of us. To the measure of our abilities we were ready to do our bits each for the little bit of scarlet on the map, and that seems to be all that is wanted. . . . But in any popular assembly, anywhere, the artist must needs feel a foreigner and lonely. He must have the feeling that not one soul of all those thousands would understand one word of what he was talking of if he really talked of the things that occupied his mind. You are a part of the mob, at times with some of the mob-psychology yourself. But if you draw into yourself and resume your individuality you are frightened. That is what it is. You are frightened. If that House knew what you were thinking of their entertainment and themselves they would tear you to pieces on the instant — precisely as a foreigner. That is the same all over the world; but it is at its worst in Anglo-Saxondom.

Indeed, in that frame of mind, Conrad was very impartial. He used to shock the writer who, as a Briton, knows nothing about his Imperial possessions, by declaring that the French were the only European nation who knew how to colonise; they had none of the spirit of Mr. Kipling's "You-bloody-niggerisms" about them, but regarded

black or tan or black and tan as all one humanity
with themselves, intermarrying, working peace-
fully side by side, and side by side, in Algerian
cafés of an evening, sitting and drinking their
apéritifs. And they provided the nigger with exactly the same *mairies*, frescoes, statuary in the
midst of jungles, representation in Paris and mad-
dening regulations for obtaining *permis de chasse*
or money from the Post Office as are provided in
any French town from Pont l'Evèque to Aigues
Mortes. That seemed to Conrad the way to colonise: and indeed one never heard of any Seces-
sionist movements in the French colonies, from
Algeria to Annam. But be that as it may, with all
his gloomily fatalistic views of the incapacity of
Anglo-Saxons as colonists other than by butchery
and the sjambok, in " Heart of Darkness " it is a
French, not a British, ship-of-war that bombards
the unanswering bush from the tepid seas of African coasts.

There wasn't even a shed there and she was
shelling the bush. . . . Her ensign dropped limp
like a rag; the muzzles of the long six-inch guns
stuck out all over the low hull; the greasy, slimy
swell swung her up lazily and let her down. In
the empty immensity of earth, sky, and water,
there she was, incomprehensible, firing into a con-
tinent. Pop, would go one of the six-inch guns;

a small flame would dart and vanish, a little white smoke would disappear, a tiny projectile give a feeble screech — and nothing happened. Nothing could happen. There was a touch of insanity in the proceeding. . . .

It was not that Conrad was markedly humanitarian; it was that he disliked waste of human effort even when it is expended in meaningless cruelty.

———

So, against the cruelties of fate, he stood up. . . . There was an occasion when the whole of the manuscript of the last instalment of "The End of the Tether" for *Blackwood's* was burnt shortly before it was due for publication. That sounds a small thing. But the instalments of *Blackwood* are pretty long and the idea of letting *Maga* miss an instalment appalled: it was the almost unthinkable crime. . . . The manuscript had been lying on the round, Madox Brown table, under a paraffin lamp with a glass reservoir, no doubt also an eighteen-forty contrivance: the reservoir had burst. . . . For a day or so it was like a funeral: then for moral support or because his writing room was burnt out, Conrad drove over to Winchelsea, to which ancient town the writer had removed. Then you should have seen Romance! It became a matter of days; then of hours. Conrad wrote;

the writer corrected the manuscript behind him
or wrote in a sentence — the writer in his study on
the street, Conrad in a two-roomed cottage that we
had hired immediately opposite. The household
sat up all night keeping soups warm. In the middle of the night Conrad would open his window
and shout, "For heaven's sake give me something
for *sale pochard;* it's been holding me up for an
hour." The writer called back, "Confounded
swilling pig!" across the dead-still, grass-grown
street. . . .

Telegrams went back and forth between ancient
Winchelsea and the ancient house of Blackwood in
Edinburgh. So ancient was that house that it was
said to send its proofs from London to Edinburgh
and back by horse-messenger. We started the
manuscript like that. Our telegrams would ask
what was the latest day, the latest hour, the latest
half-minute that would do if "The End of the
Tether" was to catch the presses. Blackwoods
answered, at first Wednesday morning, then Thurs-
day. Then Friday night would be just possible.
. . . At two in the morning the mare — another
mare by then — was saddled by the writer and the
stable boy. The stable boy was to ride to the junction with the manuscript and catch the six in the
morning mail train. The soup kept hot; the

writers wrote. By three the writer had done all that he could in his room. He went across the road to where Conrad was still at it. Conrad said, "For God's sake. . . . Another half-hour; just finishing. . . ." At four the writer looked over Conrad's shoulder. He was writing, "The blow had come, softened by the spaces of the earth, by the years of absence." The writer said, "You must finish now." To Ashford junction was eighteen miles. Conrad muttered, "Just two paragraphs more." He wrote, "There had been whole days when she had not thought of him at all—had no time." The writer said, "You absolutely must stop!" Conrad wrote on, "But she loved him, she felt that she had loved him after all," and muttered, "Two paragraphs. . . ." The writer shouted—it had come to him as an inspiration—"In the name of God, don't you know you can write those two paragraphs into the proofs when you get them back? . . ."

That was what life was like with us. At our last sitting over "Romance" we began, at the Pent, at ten in the morning. We worked solidly till dinner, not lunch time; played two games of chess, began again at nine and, just as we finished, the dilapidated Hunt fell back and dropped the kindling-faggot wood wrapped in newspaper that he was bringing in to light the fire with. . . . As for the last two paragraphs of "The End of the Tether", they never got written. Conrad disliked the story as being too sentimental and never wanted to touch it again. So the close remains, for Conrad, a trifle bald. It was to have ended with two polyphonic paragraphs in a closing rhythm — as it might be: the coming-on of an incommensurable darkness!

And then we had the Jack-ashore touch. It brought into play Conrad's incomparable business powers. The Insurance Man came to look at the blistered table and the holes in the carpet, both of which had belonged to Madox Brown. They were therefore on their last legs. The Insurance Man, a gloomy sportsman in a long overcoat, sat on a small chair, gazing at the ruins and leaning his chin on the crook of his umbrella. "It looks a very *old* carpet," he said. "Almost time the moths had it, is n't it?" "But that's just what makes its value," Conrad said. "My dear faller, consider the feet that have walked on it." "The table's very old, too," the Insurance Man said gloomily. "That's why it's so immensely valuable," Conrad said. "Consider all the people with great names that have sat round it. It's an historic table. That's what it is." "I'm afraid," the In-

surance Man said, "that we can't pay for historic
associations." "But that's just exactly what you
do have to pay for," Conrad cried. "That before
everything. Consider what you would have to pay
if Windsor Castle burned down. Yet that's most
incommodious as a residence. Dreadfully old-
fashioned." The Insurance Man shivered and
drove away more depressed than ever. . . . Eventually the Company repaired the table so that the
top shone as it can never have shone since 1840:
they replaced the carpet and paid quite a substantial sum for the historic associations.

-*-

What we did with that windfall the writer cannot remember. Perhaps we hired the amazing vehicle in which we made our first motor trip: a pink
char-à-banc on solid wooden, iron-tyred wheels,
of almost no horse power. It broke down eight times
in thirty-six miles and we pushed it hilariously up
the slightest incline. But it was a good beanfeast.
Conrad had hired that machine from the retired
master mariner who, all unconsciously, had sat to
him for "Falk." He was reputed to have become
a cannibal after the screw dropped off his vessel in
the Antarctic, drifting helpless for months. The
disappointing thing about that ride was that the
children were in no sort of a way impressed. It
was no good pointing out to them that that carriage

ran without horses; they just accepted that fact along with every other phenomenon and considered that a carriage with a horse or two was a much more spirited affair.

—✳—

We went in that vehicle through Postling, through Lyminge, Barham and Elham along the shallow depression that is the Elham Valley — past the house, about eight miles from the Pent, in which he eventually died — to Canterbury, where he lies buried. That was a happy day. We put up at the Falstaff Inn where, as they say, Chaucer stayed with his pilgrims. . . . And the happy thought of which the writer spoke at the beginning of this chapter is this. . . . Yesterday a young lady came into his office and said that she had interviewed Conrad just before — for a Kansas paper — Conrad who had never allowed himself to be interviewed. He had received her with great charm; had told her many beautiful things; the writer does not interfere with the charming young lady's story by here repeating them. . . . But he must have been just the old Conrad of the old days. And he did not have to say, *Alas! that there comes a day when all the fun of life lies in the past.* For, after lunch he had out his own car and drove the young lady all over Barham Downs, by Stelling Minnis and Upper and Lower Hardres — in the forgotten valleys of "The Inheritors" opening. From time to time he said, "This is what I like; this is what I really like in life." And he stopped the car in Postling Gap that looks over the lands of the Pent, right away over the Stour Valley that is like the end of a bowl, over the Channel, to France on a clear day. He said, "This is the view I love best in the world!" That was his last Wednesday but one and the writer hopes that he will never speak with any one who saw Conrad later.

—*—

For that is the happy memory to have. He surely could look back on life, so much of it passing in that country that he loved, and could say with his dying breath that all his reverses had been temporary but that his achievements truly had all such permanence as is vouchsafed to us men. . . . That is to be granted what we Papists call the cross of the happy death.

Appendix

APPENDIX

FOR those not dreading more emotion than the English language will bear, the writer appends what follows, which was written immediately after learning of the death of Conrad. It contains something that is not in the foregoing pages. The writer could not face its translation. It is reprinted from the *Journal Littéraire* of Paris for August 16, 1924.

L'INTELLIGENCE, a dit M. H. G. Wells, consiste dans la faculté de découvrir des relations entre des analogies éloignées. Ce pouvoir était le grand dan de mon ami . . .

J'ai écrit "mon ami" et je me mets à réfléchir . . . Pourquoi n'avoir pas écrit: "Ce grand maître qui vient de trépasser . . . " ou "Ce grand gentilhomme anglais qui *suivait la mer* . . .", ce qu'il eût préféré, lui-même?

Car, né en Pologne, au siècle dernier, il fut d'abord lieutenant de torpilleur de la marine militaire française — puis une espèce de gentilhomme anglais du siècle de la reine Elizabeth, des Drake, des Grenville — et des grands poètes, les contemporains de Shakespeare. Pour comprendre le génie de Conrad, il faut se souvenir que la civilisation polonaise s'est arrêtée vers la fin du dix-septième siècle, siècle de ses gloires guerrières et de sa chute. Et Conrad garda jusqu'à la fin de sa vie la mentalité de ce siècle de grands gentilshommes qui "suivaient la fortune sur la mer" et qui étaient des grands poètes.

La plus forte influence qui s'est fait sentir sur la vie de Conrad — sur sa vie littéraire, sur ses voyages, sur la façon dont il affronta sa carrière pénible et glorieuse — émane des romans du Capitaine Marryatt. Un grand — un très grand — romancier-marin anglais. Les livres de Marryatt parlent presque exclusivement de la guerre des frégates dans la Méditerranée du temps de Napoléon Ier . . . Et, au moment de sa mort, Conrad était en train d'écrire un roman sur ce même sujet.

"Peter Simple", "Percival Keene", "Japhet in Search of a Father", "Midshipman Easy" . . . surtout peut-être "Midshipman Easy" . . . ce sont les livres qu'il faut lire si l'on veut comprendre la simple philosophie de l'âme anglaise — et de l'âme de Conrad . . .

Quelle est la profession de foi d'un Anglais du dix-neuvième siècle? Il pense que dans les questions de marine militaire, il vaut trois — que dis-je? — sept, huit, dix-sept Français; qu'en mer, il existe seul et règne tandis que les Français restent à tout jamais ses subordonnés; que les Anglais sont les représentants du Plus Haut qui tient la mer dans le creux de sa main; que les Français, soutenus par un diable personnel, n'existent que pour être chassés de la mer, pour se cacher derrière les digues de Toulon; que tout Anglais, et surtout l'Anglais qui "suit la mer" est courageux, hautain, hardi, probe, avisé, blond, de six pieds de hauteur . . . Et cette profession de foi simpliste, Joseph Conrad Kurzeniowski, en a été imbibé à l'âge de huit ans, dans la Vologda, en lisant ses premiers romans — les romans du Capitaine Marryatt qui jouissaient d'une popularité incroyable en Pologne, de, disons, 1840 à 1870 . . . Et les derniers mots

que Conrad m'a adressés sur cette question furent justement
que Conrad restait du même avis: après Shakespeare, Marryatt
était le plus grand romancier anglais. Je venais de lui rappeler
que nos relations littéraires s'étaient nouées vingt-cinq ans
auparavant par l'expression d'une opinion identique — même
par des mots identiques . . .

L'ironique destin a voulu que ses premiers voyages se fissent
sous le pavillon français. Il parlait l'anglais jusqu'à sa mort
d'un bon accent méridional français qui le rendait presque in-
compréhensible à tout Anglais qui ne parlait pas au moins un
peu le français: il pensait, il me l'a avoué pour la dernière fois
en mai de cette année, toujours en français. Aujourd'hui il
est mort: le plus grand maître, le plus grand dompteur de ces
choses sauvages que sont les mots, les rythmes, les phrases et
les cadences de la langue anglaise — le plus grand que nos îles
aient vu . . .

Plutôt petit de taille, les épaules très larges, les bras longs,
la barbe courte et les cheveux très noirs, les dents très blanches,
doué d'une voix profonde, quand son attention était vraiment
éveillée, il insérait un monocle dans l'œil gauche et vous re-
gardait de très près . . .

Il possédait — pendant les jours de notre pauvreté commune
— une extraordinaire voiture à quatre roues, poussiéreuse, en
osier noir et une femelle quadrupède, chevaline, à longues
oreilles que tout le monde prenait pour un mulet . . . Et nous
avons passé des heures, des journées, des nuits entières, bal-
ancés, cahotés, très fiers, dans notre calèche qui roulait entre
les haies vertes et soignées, l'été, grises et en haillons épineux,
l'hiver. Et nous nous demandions sans cesse l'un à l'autre:

"Comment allez-vous 'rendre' en mots ces grands champs
de blés que sillonnent les vents faibles? . . . Comment, donc,
mon vieux Ford . . ."

Lundi passé — c'est bien aujourd'hui dimanche — je passais, balancé, cahoté, par le trot saccadé d'un quadrupède féminin septuagénaire, dans une voiture de louage quelconque, noire-grise et poussiéreuse . . . Et nous nous promenions entre les champs de blés dont les vents faibles sillonnaient les surfaces roussâtres . . . Et je me disais: c'est la vraie vérité que je me disais:

" Eh bien, mon vieux, comment allez vous 'rendre,' ces champs de blés, ces petits clos, ces petites collines vertes et ondulantes — de la France ? "

Et je continuais à y penser tout en discutant le prix de ce parcours avec le cocher vieux et sournois; tout en achetant mes billets; en achetant le *Daily Mail* que jamais, jamais de ma vie je n'acheterai plus; et même en lisant les mots: *Sudden Death of Joseph Conrad.*

Je m'occupais de la recherche des mots justes qui rendraient ces champs chuchotants et dorés . . . Et j'entendis ma voix qui criait: à ma compagne: " *Look . . . Look . . .* Regardez !" Et j'indiquais le journal qu'elle tenait et dont je pouvais lire les majuscules noires . . . *Mort soudaine de Joseph Conrad.*

Et, d'un coup, j'ai vu, s'étalant devant les bâtiments de cette gare de banlieue parisienne — j'ai vu une nuit de clair de lune dans une petite ville très ancienne qui domine là-bas la Manche. C'était sur une vérandah à toit de verre où grimpaient des vignes fanées . . . Et, dans les taches d'ombre noires, et les taches le lumière blanches, il était une heure du matin, et debout, Conrad parlait . . .

Il nous racontait comment, sous les palmiers des îles malaisiennes, assis, les jambes croisées, par terre, il enseigna, l'usage
de la machine à coudre aux petites femmes des rajahs mussul-
mans malaisiens . . . Et, dans les entreponts de son schooner
amarré au quai croulant, se trouvaient des caisses et des caisses
de fusils cachés sous les caisses de machines à coudre . . . Car
les rajahs des îles malaisiennes n'aiment guère leurs seigneurs
hollandais, et, là-bas la guerre a duré non pas cinq, mais trois
cent cinquante ans.

Et puis je m'entendis, me disant à moi-même:

" C'est le mur du silence éternel qui descend devant vous ! "

Que voulez-vous ? Je ne deviserai jamais devant des littéra-
teurs français sur le mot juste . . . La modestie m'en défend!
Et jamais je ne reverrai Joseph Conrad qui était le dernier Don
Quixote de la Manza du mot juste en Angleterre. Mettez vi
vous voulez que la jument fut sa Rossinante, les champs de
blés indescriptibles ses moulins à vent, sa voiture en osier noir le
char triomphal de son apothéose sur l'Ile . . . et moi-même
sûrement son Sancho . . . Et lui qui me disait sans cesse:

" Mon cher; c'est, notre métier, un vrai métier de chien . . .
Vous écrirez, et vous écrirez . . . Et personne, personne au
monde ne comprendra, ni ce que vous voulez dire, ni ce que
vous avez donné d'effort, de sang, de sueur. Et à la fin vous
vous direz: C'est comme si j'avais ramé toute ma vie dans un
bateau, sur un fleuve immense, dans un brouillard impénétrable
. . . Et vous ramerez et vous ramerez et jamais, jamais vous
ne verrez un poteau sur les rives invisibles pour vous dire si
vous montez le fleuve ou si le courant vous entraîne . . . et

vous connaîtrez la disette; les nuits froides, faute de couvertures; les viandes amères, et le sommeil hanté de regrets. Et vous ne trouverez jamais, jamais pendant toute votre vie, une âme pour vous dire si à la fin vous êtes le plus grand génie du monde . . . Ni non plus si vous êtes le dernier, le plus infecte descendant de . . . Ponson du Terrail . . ."